Honest. Personal. Transparent. Practical. These are words that capture the heart of *The Painful Side of Leadership*. Dr. Iorg is a man for whom I have the greatest respect. When he talks I listen. When he writes I pay attention. He has given to those called to lead a valuable and helpful guide as they seek to serve those under their watch care.

—Dr. Danny Akin
President, Southeastern Baptist Theological Seminary
Wake Forest, NC

In recent times, no one has captured the total experiences of leaders who dare to answer the call of leadership, as Dr. Jeff Iorg has done in this book, *The Painful Side of Leadership*. As a retired pastor, I wish I would've had such a resource during my thirty-seven years as pastor of the St. Stephen Missionary Baptist Church in La Puente, California. Surely, many decisions I made during those years I would have handled in a different manner. Every leader should have this book as a powerful resource, written by a man whose lif   y experiences have been chronicled for our benefit

IcCall Sr.

Pastor Emeritus, St. S   Church

uente, CA

This is a highly a   ady-to-use guide for navigating the challenges   .dership. As you continue to expand your influence and leadership capacity, you realize that practical advice, clear counsel, and godly wisdom are everyday necessities. Those are the gifts you receive in Dr. Iorg's outstanding book.

—Jack Graham
Pastor, Prestonwood Baptist Church
Plano, TX

When you lead, it sometimes feels like you are the silhouette in a shooting gallery. Everyone gets to take their shot. Other times, you cause your own problems. Either way, it hurts! Leaders of every generation face the same problems. Jeff's transparency and practical counsel will show you the way forward—even when the way forward is painful.

—Ed Stetzer
President of LifeWay Research

Saturated with seasoned wisdom and permeated with practical experience, *The Painful Side of Leadership* is a priceless treasure in any leader's library. These pages drip with invaluable counsel for walking through the inevitable valleys and eventual victories that every leader encounters. I have only been a pastor for three years, and I just wish I could have read this book three years ago! Thank you, Dr. Iorg, for giving us this gift.

—David Platt
Senior Pastor, The Church at Brook Hills
Birmingham, AL

THE PAINFUL SIDE OF LEADERSHIP

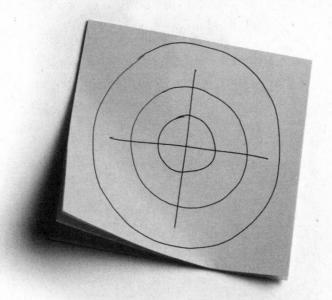

MOVING FORWARD EVEN WHEN IT HURTS

JEFF IORG

PUBLISHING GROUP
Nashville, Tennessee

978-0-8054-4870-2

Published by B&H Publishing Group,
Nashville, Tennessee

Dewey Decimal Classification: 303.3
Subject Heading: LEADERSHIP \ MANAGEMENT

Unless otherwise designated, Scripture quotations
are from the Holman Christian Standard Bible, copyright
© 1999, 2000, 2002, 2003 by Holman Bible Publishers,
Nashville, Tennessee; all rights reserved.

Passages marked NIV are from the New International
Version, copyright © 1973, 1978, 1984 by
International Bible Society.

Passages marked KJV are from the King James Version.

7 8 9 10 11 • 13 12 11 10

For Ann
Who held my hand through the longest night of my life.

Who can find a capable wife?
She is far more precious than jewels.
The heart of her husband trusts in her,
And he will not lack anything good.
Proverbs 31:10–11

Contents

Introduction

1. Why Leading Christians Is Painful   1
2. General Strategies for Managing Painful Situations   17

Painful Circumstances

3. Dealing with Disappointment   35
4. Resolving Your Mistakes   53
5. Coping with Loneliness   71
6. Living in the Spotlight   93

Painful Relationships

7. Understanding Criticism   113
8. Handling Criticism   131
9. Managing Followers in Conflict   151
10. Terminating Someone from Your Team   171

Painful Choices

11. Taking a Courageous Stand   189
12. Leading a Significant Change   209
13. Modeling a Challenging Commitment   229
14. Moving to a New Position   247

Conclusion

15. Hope—God's Gift to Hurting Leaders   265

Notes   273

Why Leading Christians Is Painful

"Hey, Jeff, do you have a minute we could talk?"

When leaders ask me that question, it's seldom because they want to share good news. They usually ask me how to handle a difficult leadership problem. Often, the situation includes a painful, personal dimension. This book is about what we discuss in those conversations.

Leading Christians is a tough job. But it just doesn't seem that it should be so difficult. The most popular biblical image for Christian leadership is a shepherd with his sheep. How pastoral! How peaceful that seems! Yet, any experienced Christian leader will tell you this contented scene is only found in the Christmas pageant—and then, only if you're lucky.

The realities are sheep bite, run amok, get diseases, wander into trouble, and are attacked by wolves. They do dumb things (even the seemingly smart ones), injure themselves (often blaming the shepherd), and nip at each other (usually some other sheep's fault). And occasionally, through no fault of their own, a storm comes up and many get hurt by circumstances no one could have anticipated or controlled.

Shepherds are also less than perfect. They get angry, desert their posts, or neglect their responsibilities. They drive their sheep, lash out at them, yell at them, and even hit a few with their staffs. And, worst of all, shepherds sometimes flirt with other herds, hoping to find greener pastures and better sheep than the ones they are stuck with tending.

The idyllic, pastoral scene illustrating Christian leadership is often merely wishful thinking. But, given our significant spiritual resources and high ideals, *why?*

God loves us, loves our followers, and wants the best for all of us. Christians want to love and obey God in return. We have clear biblical instructions on how to relate to one another, relate to those in authority over us, and relate to those we are responsible to lead. We have ample spiritual resources to empower healthy relationships. These include the filling of the Holy Spirit, instruction from the Bible, positive examples of other believers, and encouragement from living in Christian community.

We also have a shared mission that is supposed to unite us. We are responsible to fulfill the Great Commission in the spirit of the Great Commandment (Matt. 22:34–40; 28:18–20). All of us working toward the same goal should produce unity, focus, cooperation, and harmony. Besides all this, we have formal covenants, contracts, policies, and other agreements to systematize our organizational relationships.

So, with all these things going for us, *why is Christian leadership often so painful?* Here are six reasons, but by no means an exhaustive list.

Christians Still Make Sinful Choices

Becoming a Christian is a life-changing experience. When a person places faith in Jesus Christ as Lord and Savior, a new birth occurs. The old person passes away and a new person emerges because "if anyone is in Christ, there is a new creation" (2 Cor. 5:17). Despite this dramatic change, however, a residue of the old life remains. That residue is called sin. While sin is forgiven by Jesus "in whom we have redemption, the forgiveness of sins" (Col. 1:14) and the power of sin is broken at conversion (Rom. 6), all believers are still somehow infected with a propensity to sin (Rom. 7:13–25).

Thick theology books have been written to try to explain this process. Seminaries have semester-long courses, like "The Theology of Sin" or "The Doctrine of Man," to grapple with these issues. This is, by the way, one of the few subjects I consider myself an absolute authority on and completely qualified to teach. On the subject of sin, I am an expert! But while we may joke about it, our struggle with sin is a painful part of our spiritual journey and a very real part of our relationships with those we lead.

Leading Christians is painful because they do sinful things that complicate our lives as leaders, our attempts to lead them, and the organizations of which they are a part. Here, for example, are some of the bizarre choices my *Christian* followers have made.

A couple was actively working in a local county election campaign. Their opponent vandalized some of their candidate's yard signs. They decided to get even. Since the wife worked in the county courthouse, the couple conspired to tamper with the election. They voted about one hundred bogus ballots and then were so guilt ridden they confessed what they had done even before the votes were counted. They went to jail for months.

A leader was caught in an adulterous affair. When confronted he denied his actions. When presented with the evidence, he blamed his wife for being inattentive to his needs. When dismissed from his position, he claimed he had confessed and was treated without mercy. Then, to top everything, he claimed he was wrongly dismissed because state law protected his right to sexual expression. His attorney claimed the man's sexual preference was adultery, so "he couldn't be terminated for his sexual preference in this state."

We celebrated a wedding between a young man in our church and his beautiful bride. He returned from his honeymoon and started an adulterous affair. Within a year, another woman in the community claimed she was pregnant by this man. He confessed, left his wife, abandoned the pregnant woman, and moved in with a third woman.

All these situations have one thing in common—sinful choices that produced leadership pain. The choices these followers made created conflict in churches and ministry organizations. They caused people to choose sides, be publicly embarrassed, and spend hours trying to sort out the conflicts. These situations resulted in sleepless nights, many meetings (including legal briefings), and hours and hours spent in damage control and relationship repair. All these situations consumed time that could have been spent in more productive pursuits than cleaning up these messes. Yet, they happened on my watch and leading through them was part of the job.

While some painful leadership situations (like leaving for

a new ministry assignment or managing change in a growing ministry) aren't caused by sin, many are. Sin shows no sign of letting up in the Christian community. As long as our followers are sinners, painful leadership scenarios are inevitable.

Christian Leaders Are Also Sinners

Our followers' sinful choices create pain for us as leaders. Sometimes, though, we shoot ourselves in the foot (or sometimes in my case, both feet). Our sin contributes to the pain we experience as leaders. A call to Christian leadership doesn't superspiritualize a ministry leader. We still walk on clay feet. We still struggle with sin. Our choices impact our leadership effectiveness, and sinful choices can create painful circumstances. Here are two examples from my leadership hall of shame.

Our church custodian was doing a poor job. I was intimidated by her husband and didn't want the conflict of terminating her. So I determined to force her to quit. I changed her job assignment and hours in a way I knew would be unacceptable to her. She protested. I shrugged it off. She quit. Case closed. I won.

Then her husband came to see me. He threatened me physically. I was afraid to stand up lest he knock me down. So I stayed seated at my desk while he told me—his wife's boss and their pastor—what he thought of my actions. Then he told the deacons, his Sunday school class, and just about everyone else in the church (so it seemed). I maintained my innocence and justified my actions to my leaders. They gave tepid support over a few months, except for one man who had the courage to tell me the truth. I had to make it right.

Going to apologize to this couple was difficult and distasteful. My sin had to be confessed, however, and forgiveness sought. Attempting to restore the relationship was the right thing to do. But it was painful—on many levels—both public and private. I had embarrassed myself, lost credibility with my leadership team, revealed my inadequacies and insecurities in humiliating ways, disclosed myself as a weaselly schemer, and hurt the overall ministry of the church. Other than that, it really wasn't all that bad. Painful!

Another really stupid decision was having a gossipy conversation with an associate pastor—evaluating the performance of a different associate—in the hallway of our church offices. After completing the conversation, we discovered the person we were talking about was sitting in an adjoining office, listening to the entire conversation. This strategy—gossiping about someone behind his back—proved a very ineffective way to improve staff morale. My credibility was damaged, our team was fractured, trust was lost, and hours had to be spent repairing the damage. Painful!

Leadership pain can be caused by our sinful choices. We make mistakes, do dumb things, say things we wish we could take back, or otherwise reveal our sinfulness. We sin. Our followers sin. Either way, sinful choices by sinful people create leadership pain. But that's not the only way sin makes leadership painful.

Sin Infects Everything

Painful circumstances can also result from the principle of sin—not individual sins by leaders or followers but the principle of sin. The principle of sin, also called the curse of sin, is the atmospheric angst under which the entire universe struggles (see Rom. 8:18–22). When sin entered the world, it infected and affected everything. Consequently, if you feel that the world you are living in is cursed, you are right.

The curse of sin means things break down, resources run out, organizations malfunction, and cultural opposition conspires to limit or detract from our success. The curse of sin also means nature is affected. Tornadoes, earthquakes, hurricanes, fires, and other storms hit Christian ministries all the time. We are not immune to these events and the corresponding leadership hassles they cause.

For example, once our church building flooded. We lost furniture, supplies, and materials throughout the lower level. We had significant expenses—even after insurance payments—to repair building damage. During the cleanup I decided to dispose of some old church pews in the basement. It turned out they were antiques, worth thousands. I let them go for almost nothing to a junk dealer. Needless to say, the flood and my uninformed decision created painful consequences for me as a leader.

In another setting, we were building a new ministry facility when a frantic call reported, "The whole building is being flooded by the fire sprinklers." I rushed to the building, to find only four rooms affected (relief—a false report from an alarmed workman). A few months later we moved into the building. Through a design error, the first time we had freezing temperatures, the supply pipes for the fire sprinkler system ruptured. Water filled the attics, and entire ceilings throughout the facility started collapsing. Oh, how I wished this report had also been a false alarm! Drywall, light fixtures, insulation, and wiring collapsed onto desks, library shelving, computers, phone systems, and personal effects. Our brand-new building was literally falling into our laps. Decidedly not a good day!

Those events created painful leadership situations. Money had to be raised to repair the damage, decisions about legal action had to be made, forgiveness had to be sought (and given), trust/confidence was damaged, ministry momentum was lost, and time was spent solving building problems rather than doing more productive ministry. Bad things happen to good people. Bad things, things out of our control, also happen to good leaders. And when they do, they can be painful to lead through. Leadership, in times like these, is definitely needed. In fact, leaders sometimes rise to their finest hour when painful circumstances outside their control are thrust on them.

Sometimes the principle of sin, the curse on the universe, rises up and bites us. Sin, then, from various sources and in various expressions, creates pain for leaders. But sin in its myriad expressions is not the only cause of painful leadership circumstances.

Satan Is on the Prowl

The Bible teaches a cosmology (Eph. 6:10–20, for example) that includes angels, demons, and the personification of evil—Satan. Satan is described as a "roaring lion," seeking whom he can devour (1 Pet. 5:8). The devil is not in the details; he is loose in the universe like a lion prowling for fresh meat. He particularly despises Christian leaders and attacks them relentlessly, stealthily, looking for weakness and exploiting it for his destructive purposes.

How else can the fall of so many prominent Christian leaders in the past few years be explained? Yes, many made bad choices, but is that a sufficient explanation? I don't think so. There is something demonic about the circumstances when a prominent leader who has given outstanding leadership for decades suddenly implodes. The devil hates leaders and works to make them miserable. Dramatic collapse of a leader's character and ministry is visible evidence of the devil's work, but there are countless smaller skirmishes that also create pain for leaders.

There seem to be two extremes when considering how Satan is at work against us. One is to imagine the devil behind every contrary event. One person said, "If I can't find a parking place, I know the devil is trying to keep me from going to church." That seems too trivial to ascribe to Satan. The other extreme is to deny spiritual warfare and explain every conflict in purely human terms or as an unfortunate coincidence. This denies the clear teaching of Scripture.

So how do you recognize satanic opposition to your leadership? That's a complex question requiring careful spiritual discernment. While there is no foolproof formula, here are some principles to help you detect satanic opposition in leadership situations.

Satan is often behind stealthy opposition.

This includes anonymous letters or blogs, as well as spokesmen who claim, "A lot of people think . . ." It might also include well-placed misinformation or half-truths disseminated about your leadership. Some attackers have a special ability to twist words, edit comments, and compile information to distort what a leader initially meant. Confronting this kind of misinformation effectively is virtually impossible. Enduring it until it dies a natural death is often your best option.

Satan may be involved when the opposition is manipulative.

Attempts at blackmail fall into this category. For example, a favorite ploy of some is threatening leaders with the standby line, "If you don't (fill in the blank), I will stop attending/giving/supporting (or some other negative threat)." Spinning information to suit specific outcomes or ignoring the full picture the whole truth would provide are other examples of manipulation.

Satan may be involved when opposition is clandestine.

When people call secret meetings or try to bypass authority structures in decision making, be on guard. When opposition must be organized in secret, it is unlikely God is behind the effort. God works in the light, the devil in the shadows.

Satan is also behind resolutely uncooperative opposition.

Refusing to dialogue about issues or refusing to repent from sin may indicate a deep, negative spiritual force at work. This is not the normal, run-of-the-mill opposition leaders routinely face. It is entrenched negativity grounded in persistent, insidious bitterness. It is opponents who reject any possibility that they might be wrong or any opportunity for dialogue and resolution.

When these issues are the sources of leadership pain, gather your spiritual resources for the battle. You may be in for a long ordeal, and sadly, you may not prevail. Sometimes, in the short run, the devil wins. When that happens, take the long view of the promised triumph of God's kingdom. You may have lost a battle, but God will eventually win the war. Good will triumph over evil, but the ultimate victory may not happen during your tenure.

God Allows Painful Circumstances

Our focus thus far has been on negative circumstances and problems that cause pain for leaders. Sin and Satan create significant problems. But some painful circumstances are *not* the result of sin. They aren't even necessarily negative, just painful. These kinds of circumstances include things like moving to another ministry assignment, losing people who leave your ministry for another opportunity, disappointing results from a project you have poured your heart into, and challenges resulting from doing your job well. God sometimes allows challenging circumstances, not because we (or anyone else) have done anything wrong, but as part of his process of shaping us into the image of Jesus.

God has a definite purpose for you. He is intentional, even relentless, about accomplishing his purpose. God is determined to shape you into the image of Jesus. He wants to create the character of Jesus Christ in you. Your circumstances have purpose. Life is not out of control. All difficulty comes through the protective filter of God's purpose. When painful leadership circumstances arise, trust God is at work through them.

Most leaders easily forget their primary reason for being placed in their leadership role. The primary reason isn't for you to do things for God. It's so God can use your leadership setting as a laboratory for shaping the image of Jesus in you. God, who spoke a universe into existence in six days, doesn't need us to do anything for him. While he uses us, he has a greater purpose than task accomplishment. He has placed us in our unique setting because those circumstances are uniquely suited to shaping our character. As one professor was fond of saying, "Life is curriculum," and the learning outcome is the character of Jesus in us. Here is an example of this principle in a leadership situation.

Self-sufficiency, really pride by a more respectable title, has always been a problem for me. It bothers me to depend on other people. Taking responsibility, pulling myself up by my own bootstraps, is a high value for me. God wants to change this in me, to bring balance to my overzealous determination to be self-sufficient. So, he placed me in the ministry and assigned me the role of asking people for money. My livelihood my entire adult life has been dependent on gifts from others. How humbling!

One person defined my current job by joking, "A seminary president lives in a nice house on a hill and travels around the country asking for money." That isn't totally true (we don't live on a hill). God has placed me in a role with a primary job assignment that continually humbles me and breaks my self-sufficiency. It is sometimes wearisome (polite form of worry-some) to live this way financially. Yet, God has made this an ever-present part of my ministry, now and in the future. God has shaped my leadership laboratory to address my character deficiency of being too self-reliant.

What challenging, even painful, leadership circumstance is God allowing in your life right now? Are you discerning how he is shaping your character? Are you cooperating with him in the process? Are you like a fine horse, quickly responding to God's gentle direction, or are you more like a mule that has to be forced to obey? A chief spiritual discipline for leaders is discerning how God is shaping your character through the leadership challenges you encounter—and then responding positively.

Discerning how God is shaping your character is not ethereal speculation about "what God is doing in your life." Discerning God's activity is asking the question, "Father, why are you allowing this to happen to me?" and allowing enough time to pass to discover the answer. When you ask this question, your attitude is very important. Avoid asking God in an accusatory fashion, "Why is this happening to *me?*" Instead, ask humbly, seeking understanding by emphasizing "Why is *this* happening to me?" Asking rightly leads to disciplined discernment, discovering how God is shaping you into the image of Jesus, to his character revealed in the Bible.[1]

Leading Change Can Be Painful

Another reason Christian leadership is often painful is because leaders are change agents. Leadership is an influence relationship that produces real change and real change can mean real pain. We will consider the reasons change produces so much conflict and how to manage the pain in chapter 12. For now, let's just agree initiating change is a surefire way to create painful circumstances in your leadership setting.

The first time I saw the church building at my first pastorate I thought, "This church has to relocate." A few months later I suggested the idea to our church's leaders. It was like setting off a stink bomb. Faces contorted and people ran for cover. Discussion was quickly squelched. A year or so later the idea resurfaced. This time we decided to move the idea forward for public discussion by the church.

I am not sure "discussion" is the right word. A miniriot resulted. Members asked me, "Why are you taking my church from me?" and "Don't you know my children were baptized in this church?" and "Why did you come here if you don't want to pastor this church?" and "How can you do this when all my daughters were married in this church?" and "Do you think you are too good for this building?" and "Where do you think you can get the money?" and on and on. Eventually the church relocated but not before much anger was expressed and conflict resolved. Initiating a major change in your church or organization is a recipe for leadership pain.

Sometimes, unfortunately, even small changes can create difficulty. One pastor called on a Monday and said, "We moved the offering from the middle of the service to the end yesterday. I think I may survive the uproar." While we might scoff at that church's superficiality, most experienced leaders can recount similar instances of major conflict resulting from minor changes.

Christian leaders challenge people to change. We challenge them to change personally. We preach and teach, calling people to a higher standard of living, to live out their faith. We confront comfortable behavior, sometimes sinful patterns, and demand repentance. Most preachers or teachers have heard the comment, "You really stepped on my toes today." We *are* sometimes toe stompers. It comes with the territory. When people are convicted of sin, of needed life changes, they sometimes lash out in anger. Or they sulk or gossip or use a diversionary tactic (like creating conflict over unrelated issues) to distract attention from their sin. Challenging people to change is painful, as is dealing with their immature responses.

We also challenge people to change by defining the future and inspiring people to help create it. We challenge people to attempt new ministries, build new facilities, and take risks (like going overseas on mission trips). These kinds of challenges also create tension, healthy tension, but still uncomfortable pressure as people struggle with growth and change.

Leaders even choose to promote growth by causing painful circumstances. One man accepted a small-church pastorate. A denominational leader visited and offered to help the church with money and personnel to inject immediate new energy into the church. The pastor declined, saying, "We need to do this ourselves." He knew turning down the assistance would create pain in the short run, but he also knew his parishioners would grow through the pain of struggling to improve their own facility and ministries. Mature leaders initiate change, accept the pain that comes with it, and allow the process to do its maturing work among their followers.

Conclusion

In summary, why is Christian leadership often a painful process? On the negative side, we are sinful people leading sinful people. The devil is real and working hard to oppose us. Our world system is sin cursed. This means bad things will happen to good people, including well-meaning Christian leaders. Life happens and it's often messy.

On the positive side, doing our job well can also produce painful circumstances. Churches grow, ministries expand, and people change. Success means change, and change usually means pain for someone. Also, God sometimes allows painful circumstances—like a flood or a fire—over which we have no control. God always has a plan for our "welfare, not for disaster" (Jer. 29:11). His plan is to shape the character of Jesus Christ in us through the leadership circumstances he allows.

This book describes many painful situations and encourages you to accept them as part of your leadership assignment and learn to lead through them. Denial isn't healthy. Dropping out isn't an option. We are called to lead and lead we must, through pain, through difficulty, and through opposition. We must lead even when it hurts.

2

General Strategies for Managing Painful Situations

Painful circumstances are inevitable for leaders. Whether they emerge from negative causes (like sin, Satan, or bad choices) or more positive reasons (like ministry success and growth), painful circumstances will be part of your leadership experience. They can't be avoided. They can, however, be expected, confronted, managed, and when possible, resolved. This book identifies specific problem areas and corresponding actions you can take to deal with them. Before plunging into those specific issues, however, let's consider some *general strategies* for managing painful leadership circumstances. These life practices may help you in other areas as well, but all will specifically improve your ability to lead through difficult times. These strategies are the backdrop for the more specific counsel in the rest of the book.

Have Realistic Expectations

Leaders must have realistic expectations of themselves, the people they lead, and results they can achieve. Some leaders have an unrealistic self-appraisal and are therefore continually frustrated with their progress. Some leaders inaccurately appraise the potential of their followers. And some leaders have unrealistic expectations of what can actually be accomplished in their ministry setting. Any of these flawed perspectives can produce painful breakdowns in relationships with followers, especially when a leader lashes out in disappointment-fueled anger.

Disappointment results from unmet expectations, not from actual performance (an idea expanded in greater detail in chapter 3). For example, if you planned to create ten new Bible study groups in your church this year and you created only six, how would you feel? Many leaders would be disappointed, focusing on the unmet goal rather than celebrating six new Bible studies. Avoiding disappointment requires managing your expectations, learning to walk the fine line between expecting too much of your followers (and yourself) and giving in to the status quo. When you expect too much, you will be perpetually discouraged. When you expect too little, lethargy sets in, leading to lost hope. Either extreme often expresses itself angrily—sometimes subtly, other times more publicly.

While serving as a pastor, I once went through a period of anger toward the church. The problem? The members weren't responding to my ideas, moving as rapidly as I thought they should, and doing as much as I insisted was required. In short, they weren't meeting my expectations, were making me look bad, and weren't helping me achieve renown for ministerial success. That's as painful for me to write as it was for them to live through.

After a few weeks of anger seeping into my sermons, a trusted friend asked, "What's wrong?" "Nothing," I lied. "Well," he continued, "it sure seems like something is bothering you. Every sermon feels like an attack—like you are taking us to task for something we've done to you. I'm just wondering if I can help." That cut deeply. But I knew he loved me and wanted the best for me. He wasn't accusing me, just making an insightful observation and trying to help his pastor.

This kind of leader-inflicted pain is common when a leader feels disappointed, then becomes angry because of unmet expectations. When a leader vents this kind of anger on his followers, even more pain usually results. Since "man's anger does not accomplish God's righteousness" (James 1:20), no good can come from this kind of attack. So one crucial step in managing painful leadership circumstances is having realistic expectations about yourself and your followers. Taking out your frustrations on people you blame for disappointing you never helps.

Admittedly, there is tension related to our expectations of our followers. Leaders envision the future and believe God can work through them and their followers to accomplish much more than has previously been attempted or accomplished. Leaders have vision. They see the invisible and dream the impossible. They challenge people to go beyond themselves, to trust God to do through them what they can't do by themselves. This is distinctive of Christian leadership. We lead by faith, believing God for what doesn't exist.

Many leaders have a bigger vision than can be assimilated and lived by their followers. When leaders lose touch with this reality, they become angry and their followers become frustrated. The leader's challenge is to maintain a healthy tension between vision and reality, between what can be and what is. Leaders must plan for the best, expect the worst, and adjust to what actually happens.

While this is challenging (and can be painful) on a corporate level, it is even more difficult on a personal or individual level. It's one thing to have realistic expectations about yourself and your ministry setting, in general. It's quite another challenge to maintain realistic expectations of individuals you are trying to lead without becoming discouraged (or even cynical) by their response.

People will disappoint you. One Christian leader jokingly told me, "I am a one-point Calvinist. I believe in the absolute, total, abject depravity of man. That's one absolute I'm sure of." After leading for more than thirty years, I agree with his conclusion! People are sinners and will act like it, often at times you weren't expecting and in ways you wouldn't have predicted. Having a realistic view of people, as saved sinners still infected with sinful tendencies, is essential to effective leadership. Remember this key point: Christians, even your most dedicated followers, still have a propensity to sin. And they will occasionally act out that tendency. The challenge is avoiding cynicism—being realistic without losing heart.

Acknowledging the truth about people doesn't mean we think the worst of them, expect the worst from them, or believe the worst about them. It simply means we are realistic, measured in our appraisal of their character and ability to make good choices. Leaders are optimists who want the best for people and from people. We challenge them to rise above their baser instincts and live changed lives.

But while we expect the best, we must not be surprised by the worst. When a colleague commits adultery, an employee steals money, a member becomes a gossip, or a teacher promotes heresy—we shouldn't be shocked. We know these behaviors can, do, and will happen in the Christian community. We are braced for them and prepared to lead through them. Again, we expect the best but aren't surprised by the worst. Balance hopeful vision with honest reality about the behavior you expect from your followers.

We must also have realistic expectations of "the ministry." Some persons enter ministry expecting a perpetual spiritual retreat only to find it's mostly a lot of work. Most ministry organizations are production facilities, not retreat centers. We have work to do—the hard work of making disciples. That isn't a simple or easy job. It's demanding because it's people intensive. It's draining and exhilarating—sometimes on the same day, even in the same moment. Having realistic expectations, both of our followers and our work, will go a long way in helping us cope with the painful side of leadership.

Manage Your Emotions

Leaders are usually passionate men and women. We feel deeply. Our work and our followers matter a great deal to us. We are emotionally connected to the people we lead. We love them, not in a superficial or maudlin way, but genuinely. Christian leadership involves sacrifice. We know this when we accept our calling and are more than willing to expend ourselves for the good of our followers and the advance of God's kingdom. But expending ourselves leads to emotional depletion. Tired people, even tired Christian leaders, are susceptible to frustration and depression. Emotional depletion makes us vulnerable to being controlled by negative emotions.

Perhaps the most troublesome emotion for leaders to manage is anger. Why do leaders get angry? Anger is caused by threat or a perceived threat. When we feel threatened, whether the threat is real or imagined, we often lash out in anger. Threats to our self or personhood can take many forms. For example, when someone cuts you off in traffic, your physical self is threatened so you yell in anger. When someone treats your child unfairly, your extended self is threatened and you react angrily. When someone makes fun of your weight or the size of your nose, your self-esteem is threatened and you feel angry.

In leadership situations, when someone questions your decisions, your professional identity may feel threatened. When a person opposes your vision, your dreams (an extension of who you are) may feel threatened. When a person criticizes your family, your extended self comes under attack. All these examples illustrate this principle: Anger is a response to threat or perceived threat. Lowering our threat level through developing security in Jesus Christ is essential for leaders. The security of the believer must become a personal reality, not simply a doctrine to debate.

Sometimes the pain we feel in leadership relationships is caused by our angry reactions to the sins of others and the trouble they cause us. That reaction is often rooted in the complications the actions cause, not because of the sin itself. For example, when a deacon was accused of child abuse, one leader's first reaction was, "I can't believe he did this to our church." He was more angry the sin had been discovered, and he would have to deal with its implications in the church than he was that a child had been violated. That was misplaced anger!

Anger is not the only emotion leaders struggle to manage—merely the most troublesome. We also struggle with fear, discouragement, and a nagging sense of inadequacy. We deal with grieving people and often don't acknowledge our grief and properly work through the associated emotions. This emotional depletion can lead to depression, blue Mondays that linger day after day without respite. Learning to manage our emotions, to take care of ourselves so we have something to offer others, is a required discipline for ministry leaders.

Leaders must also learn to manage, even encourage, positive expressions of emotion. It's fun to celebrate! Some leaders don't allow for much happiness around them. "This is serious business" is their attitude as they project a joy-killing sterility about their work. These leaders need to learn to manage their emotions at the other end of the scale from anger, fear, and discouragement. They need to learn to enjoy the success and progress they experience, to revel in God's blessing and celebrate achievements he enables.

I once recounted a ministry success to a mentor and then said, "Now we are . . ." He cut me off. "Wait a minute," he asked, "when are you going to lead your church to celebrate their achievement?" That was a great question. I was embarrassed to admit, until that moment, it had never occurred to me to lead anyone to celebrate anything. Accomplishments were just boxes to check on my endless to-do list—nothing more.

Managing emotions means you acknowledge negative emotions like anger and learn to express them appropriately. It also means you allow positive emotions to flow, to enjoy life with your followers. Managing your emotions means you are transparent without being cathartic, acknowledging both the highs and lows you experience as a leader. But it also means you aren't controlled by your emotions. You value emotions, good and bad feelings, as part of life—but they are not the determining factor in your behavior.

Learning to manage your emotions requires spiritual discipline and psychological stability. It isn't denying or suppressing emotions, but learning to acknowledge them and their appropriate role in relationships. Making choices about your emotions reveals maturity. Value your feelings but trust something deeper—Spirit-empowered, willful, personal choice—to control your actions as a leader. The next section outlines healthy disciplines that help maintain emotional equilibrium.

Practice Spiritual Disciplines

Leaders are busy people. It is not uncommon for a leader who is depressed, stressed-out, or emotionally empty to realize part of his pain comes from lost intimacy with God. One cause of this is forsaking the practice of basic spiritual disciplines. Managing painful leadership circumstances is, at the core, a spiritual challenge. Psychological gymnastics, clever coping mechanisms, and "one, two, three" formulas simply won't sustain you. You need something more substantial. You need a consistent, disciplined, focused lifestyle of personal devotion.

Some leaders neglect spiritual disciplines when times are good and are driven to practice them only when trouble comes. Not a good plan! Spiritual disciplines are like weight training. A football player lifts weights consistently, day after day, working hard during the off-season to build strength. During the season the hard work done previously pays off. When it's game time and the stress is on, strength is available from past disciplined training. The same is true for leaders. If you want to call on spiritual resources during difficult times, you need to build spiritual strength through disciplined practice when times are good.

The first core spiritual discipline for leaders is daily Bible reading. Reading the Bible on a regular basis, with a goal of daily reading, is essential. Why? It opens you to incremental instruction from God. He can instruct, correct, encourage, and rebuke as needed. Daily Bible reading means you encounter truth regularly, and bring your life into line as needed. A brick house is built one brick at a time. A disciplined life is built one day at a time. When you neglect your daily Bible reading, you will drift slowly from God. When correction comes, it may require significant response or repentance. How much better it would be for you to connect with God daily, so he can shape your life a little at a time, rather than through abrupt correction after you have drifted far from him.

A second core discipline is daily prayer. Most leaders pray for others more than for themselves. It is good to pray for others. But leaders also need quiet times of personal prayer— for intimate needs, for personal struggles, for issues known only to you and God. Leaders who pray this way bare their souls to God, crying out to him without reservation. They are comfortable on their knees, telling God everything. No holds barred, nothing held back. This kind of devotional prayer reconnects us with God on a personal basis, as Father, not as supervisor. Task-oriented leaders need this kind of prayer experience as a regular reminder of God's love, acceptance, and support. New perspective is found on the painful circumstances you are enduring when you openly pray through these issues and entrust them to God.

Another key discipline for leaders is Sabbath rest. You may be thinking, *Yeah, right. What planet are you living on?* As a younger leader, I thought the same thing. But God (and some good deacons) confronted me about my workaholism and God's pattern of Sabbath rest. God lays out a clear pattern (even for busy Christian leaders) of working six days and resting one. He expects us to follow his model.

Over the years this has taken different forms in our family, depending on our jobs and the ages of our children. But my wife and I have been able to rest (disengage from our work of ministry) one day per week for about forty-five weeks per year for more than twenty-five years. We found ways to do it when our children were small, and now we are doing it as empty nesters. At first, we felt guilty for shirking our duty—not working all the time. But then we discovered two realities. One, God does more through us in six days (when we are more rested and focused) than we previously did in seven. Two, resting requires us to trust God and demonstrates to our followers we really don't believe it all depends on us. Both lessons have served us well for more than twenty-five years.

Why is this so important? Because fatigue has a way of building, of gaining momentum like the proverbial snowball headed downhill. The longer you stay *on*, the deeper the fatigue settles into your soul. Tired leaders have no emotional, physical, or spiritual reserves when faced with an unexpected, difficult leadership problem. Deep fatigue, being bone tired, can have two very bad consequences for leaders when they go through painful leadership situations.

First, tired leaders make bad decisions. One leader was dismissed for falsifying his church ministry expense reports. When asked why he did it, he said, "The church demanded so much. I thought they owed it to me." He hadn't taken a full day off from his church in years. He made a series of bad choices to fake travel and bill the church because of fatigue. That isn't an excuse, just a fact. Tired leaders, particularly when the added stress of unexpected painful circumstance comes into play, often make bad decisions.

Second, tired leaders are headed for burnout and depression. Clinical depression is more than just having a bad day or a bad week. Depression is when your emotional fatigue is so profound, it impacts your capacity for meaningful relationships and appropriate performance of job duties. Leaders who become depressed usually get that way because of overwork and overcommitment leading to burnout, which spirals into depression. When we ignore God's pattern of habitual rest, of disengaging from our work (even the work of ministry), we make ourselves vulnerable. A difficult situation arises (or a series of them badly timed), and since we are spiritually and emotionally depleted, we are unable to manage the pain.

Other disciplines are important for leaders—Scripture memory, fasting, and solitude to name a few. All of these are important to maintaining a vibrant spiritual life prepared to handle the painful side of leadership. Why the focus here on daily Bible reading, daily prayer, and Sabbath rest? Because these are the first casualties of an overcommitted life and the foundation on which the other disciplines are built. When leaders are not regularly reading the Bible, praying, and resting, it is unlikely they are memorizing Scripture, fasting, practicing solitude, or any other spiritual discipline.

How are you doing? Or more specifically, what did you learn in your Bible reading *today?* What did you pray about, personally, *today?* What day, this week, will you turn off your cell phone, disconnect your e-mail, put the home phone on the answering machine, and disengage from your leadership responsibilities? Answer these questions honestly, and you may discover you are drifting from the core spiritual disciplines that will sustain you during painful leadership experiences.

Assemble a Prayer Team

Leaders are often lonely (we will consider that issue more fully in chapter 5). When trouble comes, it's particularly unsettling to look around and find yourself alone. Then it's too late to build the support team you need to get you through the tough time. Over the years there are several kinds of people who have helped sustain me as a leader. It has taken some work, but I have assembled a support team that stands with me in good times and bad.

The kinds of people who support me can be grouped in four general categories—prayer partners, mentors/counselors, peers/colleagues, and friends/supporters. In chapter 5 we will go into the last three areas in more detail. But for now let's focus on assembling one important component to every leader's success—a prayer team.

The urgency of developing my prayer team coincided with my call to leave pastoral ministry and accept a position as a denominational executive. Several issues connected with the change really concerned me—extensive travel (and the accompanying temptations), protection of and effective parenting for my young children, my ignorance of how to do my new job, and the burden of my decisions now impacting thousands of people across a multistate region. I felt undone, suddenly very small and powerless in the face of so many challenges. I knew I needed to pray. I also knew I needed people to pray for me.

Part of my new job was writing a monthly column for our newspaper. So one month I wrote about my need for prayer and invited prayer warriors—men and women who were already praying for me or would commit to praying for me—to contact me. About fifty people responded. Some of their letters were amazing.

One letter came from Cal Poncho Sr. Mr. Poncho scrawled a handwritten letter in shaky print. He wrote, "I have never met you. I saw a picture of your young family in the newspaper when you were elected our leader. I knew the pressures you would face, and I have been praying for you *every day* since then. Please put me on the prayer team." Mr. Poncho was in his eighties at that time. He was already praying for me even though we had never met! That was the kind of prayer partner I was looking for. We put Mr. Poncho on the prayer team, and he continued to pray for me *every day* for more than ten years.

Several others have also been with me from the beginning—Doris, Alice, Keith, Joe, and Earl come to mind. Some like Don and Gwen have passed away but not before standing with me *daily* for years. How humbling it is to have people, some who have never met me or only know me casually, to take up the spiritual responsibility of praying for my family and me.

Every month, since the prayer team's inception in 1995, I have written a prayer letter to this important support group. It's a simple letter. It summarizes needs for each member of our family, recounts answers to prayer in the past month, and has a list of major events on my schedule for the upcoming month. When I stand to preach or walk into an important meeting, it is empowering to know the prayer team prayed *that day* for me. I often feel like Moses whose stamina failed, but had Aaron and Hur to hold him up to sustain Joshua in battle (see Exod. 17:10–16). A prayer team doesn't undercut your need to pray, but it does sustain you and augment your prayer life.

If you think you can make it through the spiritual minefield of leadership today without serious, focused prayer by people who have a special ministry of intercession, you are arrogant and foolish. Blunt—but true! You need prayer support, prayer covering. You need supernatural protection through the prayers of others. You are too inconsistent (if you are like the rest of us) to depend only on your prayer life to sustain you.

Get a prayer team, now! Start small. Recruit people who already have the ministry of intercession. This is not a "you all come" program. You are looking for the quiet few who mean business. You are looking for people like my friend Mary who has a prayer notebook labeled "The War on the Floor." That's the kind of person you need on your prayer team. Get them organized and praying for you and your family. You will sense the difference immediately, and you will really feel the difference when tough times come.

Focus on God's Kingdom Purposes

Rick Warren famously wrote, "It's not about you."[2] That is a startling discovery for many people—even some believers. Christian leaders can easily fall into the trap of thinking their leadership roles and ministry assignments are about them—their happiness, their fulfillment, or their agenda. When we fall into that trap, we can be frustrated if our leadership assignment is difficult or painful. After all, we are serving God. Aren't we supposed to be blessed, happy, and fulfilled? Don't some media preachers tell us the center of God's will guarantees blessing—even financial riches?

Leadership in the trenches of day-to-day ministry isn't like that at all. So, what gives? Are all of us who go through intensely painful ministry leadership situations out of God's will? No.

An honest look at leadership situations in the Bible reveals the opposite is more likely to be true. God's best leaders seem to go from crisis to crisis. Consider Moses. Do you think confronting Pharaoh ten times was easy? Then he was instrumental in slaughtering thousands of Egyptians at the Red Sea. (How would you have slept that night?) Afterward, he led Israel while the people whined about food and water, travel conditions, and lack of the comforts of home. Moses had the euphoric experience of meeting God and receiving the Law, followed closely by the shocking incident with Aaron and the golden calf. After all that, he had the "privilege" of leading Israel for forty years of wilderness wandering and then was not allowed into the Promised Land. He died in sight of the goal.

Early church leaders had similar experiences. Paul, for example, was physically assaulted, personally attacked, and imprisoned for years. He faced innumerable hardships because of his leadership role (see 2 Cor. 11:22–33). Nothing in Paul's writings hints he thought his trying circumstances indicated he was out of God's will. On the contrary, the more effective his leadership, the more difficulty he seemed to encounter. God had larger purposes for Moses and Paul than their happiness or fulfillment. His purposes included developing their character and accomplishing his mission. He has the same overarching agenda for you.

Moses was a godly man, yet his leadership was marked with trouble, heartache, and strife. He led whiners and complainers. He made progress toward the ultimate goal but didn't get to share the final victory. Sounds a lot like organizational leadership today, doesn't it?

Paul was a spiritual man, yet his leadership was marked by conflict, turmoil, and debate. He led both faithful and unfaithful men and women. He made progress in his mission with mixed results. Sounds a lot like church leadership today, doesn't it?

God has a kingdom agenda—shaping the character of Jesus in his followers (including leaders) and getting the gospel to the nations. His agenda will not be thwarted, and his ways are often mysterious. Hard times aren't necessarily a sign of God's blessing or cursing. They are simply a part of kingdom leadership. Often we want the easy way. But God seems to advance his work through those who choose a harder path. How else do you explain the reality that martyrdom advances the kingdom in dramatic ways? God is at work, often through—not around—our painful leadership circumstances. When you are going through a hard time, ask God to lift your eyes from the fray to the horizon of his ultimate, eternal purposes. Leaders must take the long view, the principled view, and make decisions accordingly. Often that is a painful choice.

One young couple works in the city dump of Managua, Nicaragua. They have started a school. Many of their students already have AIDS, have been sexually assaulted, and come from horribly dysfunctional family situations. When asked how they endure this difficult place, they replied, "We have to make a little difference in this generation so the future can be different." They don't know if they will change the dump culture in their lifetime, but they believe they can catalyze a movement that will transform the dump in the next generation.

Another friend is wandering in central Asia, making contact with nomadic people who have never heard of Jesus. Most have never seen an Anglo person. His life is hard, but he has the long view. If he can break down the walls for the gospel, even if the progress is limited in this generation, perhaps the next generation will respond in droves.

These stories inspire us, but the reality is that ministry leadership is hard, at one time or another, in every setting. When you start feeling sorry for yourself, thinking it's not fair or it's too hard—refocus on kingdom purposes. God's ultimate purpose isn't your happiness. An easy life for his followers isn't his agenda. He is determined to expand his kingdom. He will not be dissuaded. And that will sometimes be painful for those of us who have volunteered to be on the front lines of spiritual leadership.

Conclusion

With these general strategies as a backdrop, let's turn our attention to specific painful situations for ministry leaders and discover insight into meeting these significant challenges. While you might not be experiencing all of these problems right now, you will encounter one or more of them eventually. And even if you are not struggling with one of these issues now, keep this book in mind as a guide or reference for solving future painful problems as they arise.

Dealing with painful situations, particularly when they aren't our fault, can be discouraging. When discouragement mounts, a profound sense of disappointment can settle on you like a London fog. Finding a way out of the haze is essential. As we begin considering specific painful leadership dilemmas, let's start with a common challenge—dealing with disappointment.

3

Dealing with Disappointment

How do you feel when you pour your whole heart into a project or a person and the results simply don't measure up to your expectations? Disappointed! It's particularly painful when you are *sure* God directed you toward a specific goal. You may find yourself questioning your competence and capacity to hear from God, as well as your leadership ability. One pastor worked for several months preparing his church for a $20-million building campaign. The church had a history of financial success, he was at the peak of a long tenure, and the church was healthy by every known measurement. He was sure of the goal, confident in the campaign process and leaders, and believed God directed them to do it. Yet only $6 million was pledged. While most of us would be *thrilled* by raising that much money, he was disappointed.

Disappointment is a result of unmet expectations, not measuring of actual performance. If you were expecting one hundred teenagers at a youth event and only fifty showed up, you would probably be disappointed. Never mind that fifty teenagers were positively impacted. The discrepancy between what we hope for and what happens is the "expectation gap." It's the feeling the bottom has dropped out from under you, that sinking feeling you get when life isn't measuring up to what you hoped for.

It can happen with events and projects but also with people. We expect people to respond and change as we minister to them. I once met a man weekly, for more than a year, trying to help him improve his ministry skills. When we were together, he seemed responsive. But he was like the Pillsbury Doughboy. When I was pressing him, he would feel the impact and promise to change. But when I left, he reverted to his former habits. My investment in him made an impression, but no permanent change resulted. After a year, I gave up—disappointed and frustrated I had spent so much time with a person who was ultimately unwilling to change.

Unmet expectations can also produce feelings of failure. As a leader, you have probably achieved a measure of success in some endeavor—whether it's with a project or a person— but because all your expectations weren't met, you felt like a failure. Feelings of failure (just like disappointment) often result from perceived levels of success or accomplishment, rather than by measuring actual performance.

The first time I was asked to speak on dealing with disappointment and failure, the request took a humorous turn. A college group, with no money to pay a speaker, invited me. Attempting to compliment me and convince me to come at my expense, the leader said, "We really want you to come. You are a good speaker. We think you can really help us deal with a difficult subject for students. We think you are perfect for this subject—how to handle failure."

How encouraging! I was the perfect speaker because I was a failure expert. I had a good time teasing the leader, and later the group, on his smooth approach to convince me to come by labeling me the Failure Expert. What a compliment!

But frankly, when I received his invitation, I felt more like a failure than he realized. My level of ministerial disappointment was at an all-time high. I was, at the time, a church planter—need I say more?

The new church had set an attendance goal of two hundred for the first worship service. We spent a lot of money, invested a huge amount of time, and prayed hard for the results. Only ninety-two people showed up the first Sunday, and then only sixty came back the second week. At that rate, I thought, *We will be out of business in two more Sundays.* We had worked hard, prayed much, and invested thousands of dollars with disappointing results.

We then revised our goal to have two hundred attendees on Easter Sunday—about six months later. Again, we worked, prayed, and gave all we had to the effort. Only about one hundred twenty-five showed up. More disappointment! It was more than two years of hard work and prayer before we finally reached our attendance goal of two hundred.

Throughout those two years, there were many disappointing events, outreach projects, evangelism efforts, and ministry projects. The worst one was Banker's Day. It was so bad, I won't write the details lest you attempt something similar, convinced you can make a bad idea work. Banker's Day was a complete failure. Not one single person came. Not one. Nada. Nobody. Zero. Zilch. A complete goose egg.

Disappointing circumstances, as defined in this chapter, include instances when you have done your best—with a project or a person—and had less-than-hoped-for results. These are instances when you followed God's plan as best you understood it, with poor results. This doesn't include circumstances you caused by poor leadership decisions or sinful choices. This chapter is about what happens when you do your best, with pure motives, to find and do God's will, but the results leave you disappointed.

Leadership mistakes—sinful choices or just bad decisions—are another matter. We will consider how to handle those in the next chapter. Sometimes leaders make sinful choices. At other times, leaders make poor decisions. In those cases, our response is very different from simply handling discouraging or disappointing results. For now, we aren't considering those types of situations. We are, instead, focusing on what to do when you have done your best and been disappointed. Here are some insights to help you with this struggle.

You're in Good Company

The Bible has numerous examples of people who made good choices, did their best, followed God as best they knew how, and found themselves in disappointing circumstances—none more dramatic than Job. Job was described as "a man of perfect integrity, who feared God and turned away from evil. . . . Job was the greatest man among all the people of the east" (Job 1:1, 3). God allowed him to be tested in dramatic fashion. He lost his family and estate through a series of natural disasters and enemy raids (vv. 13–19), none of which was his fault. Job responded with profound disappointment and deep grief when he "tore his robe and shaved his head. He fell to the ground and worshiped" (v. 20).

Job cried out to God, "Naked I came from my mother's womb, and naked I will leave this life. The LORD gives, and the LORD takes away. Praise the name of the LORD" (v. 21). Despite his painful lament, his underlying attitude is revealed by the conclusion: "Throughout all this Job did not sin or blame God for anything" (v. 22).

Job's example reveals several key principles. First, God allows profoundly disappointing circumstances, even in the lives of his most devoted followers. Second, those losses can be very personal—involving even our children or livelihood. Third, it's appropriate to express deep grief, to be honest about our feelings of loss. Job's ripping his robe and shaving his head might look different today—tears and heartfelt prayers come to mind. However it's shown, expressing deep grief is a normal response to a devastating loss. Fourth, crying out to God is part of accepting loss. Sometimes we sanitize our responses to painful circumstances. Honesty with God is better. Sprawling before God and crying out to him admits our desperation in the face of overwhelming disappointment.

My daughter went through a yearlong health crisis when she was sixteen. In eight weeks she deteriorated from a multisport, all-conference athlete to being unable to walk up stairs without assistance. She spent most of the year in bed or in a doctor's office. During the worst of it, in a desperate moment, my prayers stopped being polite "God help Melody" prayers and became agonizing cries to God for healing. Deep disappointment evokes passionate praying.

One fifth and final insight stands out from Job's experience. He cried out to God, but somehow still had faith to affirm God's providence and goodness. He prayed, "The LORD gives, and the LORD takes away. Praise the name of the LORD" (v. 21). No matter how unfair your situation, how tragic your circumstances, how disappointed you feel (with God, yourself, or people), God can be trusted. Affirm your confidence in him. Celebrate his goodness. Trust his providence. Like Job, determine to "praise the name of the Lord" despite your painful circumstances.

God Is at Work in All Circumstances

Every time something disappointing happens, God is still at work. Prosperity-gospel advocates teach God is uniquely present in good times, and success is proof of his presence and blessing. The Bible has another message. God is with believers at all times, working in every circumstance.

Romans 8:28–29 promises, "We know that all things work together for the good of those who love God: those who are called according to His purpose. For those He foreknew He also predestined to be conformed to the image of His Son." *All things* mean all things—an unequivocal promise from God. God is at work through all circumstances to fulfill his ultimate purpose of conforming each and every believer to the image of Jesus Christ. *All* means all.

That is very good news! God works through your disappointing circumstances. Some ask, "Does God cause or allow disappointing circumstances?" While debating the answer might be theologically stimulating, does it really matter? Either way, God is behind the circumstances he causes or allows.

Either way, God oversees every situation and has purpose in it. Either way, he has mysterious power to coordinate an infinite number of variables throughout the universe, simultaneously, to accomplish his purpose in the life of each and every believer. God is amazing—a loving Father who accomplishes his purpose in your life by using every circumstance for good.

Joseph is one biblical character who expressed this principle to make sense of a difficult, painful situation. Joseph had been sold into slavery, falsely accused of rape, and imprisoned before finally rising to leadership in Egypt. He lived in isolation from his family for many years. Soon after reuniting with them, his father died. His brothers, who had sold him into slavery, feared retribution (see Gen. 37; 39–50).

But Joseph told his brothers, "You planned evil against me; God planned it for good" (Gen. 50:20). When circumstances out of your control wreck your dreams, it takes spiritual discipline to affirm God's purpose and plan. God is at work through your circumstances, all your circumstances. Affirming, by faith, God's providence and overarching reason for your circumstances is foundational to your spiritual growth and development. Remember, *all* means all. This certainly doesn't mean all your circumstances are good, only that God will accomplish a good purpose through them.

Making this affirmation "What seems intended for evil, God will use for good in my life" reflects spiritual maturity. It isn't always easy to discern how God is working or why he has allowed your disappointing circumstances. But the difficulty you may have in discerning God's work or ways doesn't invalidate the fact of God's promise. *All* means all.

While it's impossible to create a comprehensive list of how God works through disappointing circumstances, here are some examples of ways leaders can be shaped toward the image of Jesus through times of pain and loss.

Our Disappointments Share the Sufferings of Jesus

Jesus suffered in ways we aren't able to comprehend, much less experience. He suffered for the sins of the human race while we suffer only for our sins or perhaps the sins of someone whose actions harm us. He suffered physically while many Christians seldom are more than inconvenienced for their faith. He chose to suffer while most of us do all we can to avoid pain. Paul wrote, "For it has been given to you on Christ's behalf not only to believe in Him, but also to suffer for Him" (Phil. 1:29). Peter added, "But if anyone suffers as a Christian, he should not be ashamed, but should glorify God with that name. . . . So those who suffer according to God's will should, in doing good, entrust themselves to a faithful Creator" (1 Pet. 4:16, 19). Jesus' suffering is unique, yet believers are called to share it. How can you do this?

One way is to suffer unjustly, to do the right thing with the right motive and then be criticized, attacked, or punished for it. When this happens, you will feel disappointed—to say the least! Jesus suffered but with no responsibility for causing the suffering. When you do your best and suffer for it, you share with Jesus (in some small way) the same kind of injustice he experienced. This is one way to share the sufferings of Jesus.

One pastor discovered a deacon was involved in a white supremacy organization. He confronted the man and asked him to either renounce his affiliation or resign his church leadership position. He refused on both counts. The pastor then took the matter to the church's leaders, only to be rebuffed in his efforts to have the deacon removed from a leadership role. The pastor then asked publicly for either the deacon's resignation or removal from office by vote of the church. The church stood with the pastor and removed the erring leader but not without serious consequences. Families left the church. Finances struggled. The pastor's family experienced hostility in their small community. Eventually they were forced to leave. Sometimes, when you do the right thing, you suffer for it.

Another way you may experience the disappointment associated with Jesus' sufferings is to invest in people who fail you. Jesus wasn't always "successful" if success is measured by the behavior of some of his hand-selected followers. He chose Judas after an all-night prayer meeting (Luke 6:12). Judas later betrayed Jesus (Luke 22:47–48). Jesus took Peter, James, and John with him for spiritual support in Gethsemane. They slept while he agonized (Matt. 26:36–46). Contemporary leaders are often disappointed when a follower is unfaithful to a program or a project. Think how much more serious were the failures of Jesus' followers. They failed him at crucial moments related to his crucifixion. Jesus chose some followers who disappointed him. You will do the same and in a small way share the sufferings (and disappointments) of Jesus.

Our Disappointments Reveal Misplaced Affections

When people let you down, it may reveal how much you are depending on others to meet your deepest needs. Christian leaders, like all believers, are susceptible to subtle idolatry. We can look to people, activities, accomplishments, money, or other false sources of spiritual satisfaction. When we depend on anyone other than Jesus to satisfy our deepest needs, we will be disappointed.

Colossians 3:1–2 challenges us, "If you have been raised with the Messiah, seek what is above, where the Messiah is, seated at the right hand of God. Set your minds on what is above, not on what is on the earth." Another translation of the last sentence is "Set your minds on things above, not on earthly things" (v. 2 NIV). But my favorite translation is "Set your *affection* on things above, not on things on the earth" (v. 2 KJV, emphasis added).

Leaders want to feel successful. We want people to like us. We want admiration for our accomplishments. None of these desires is inherently wrong. God made us relational and creative. We work with people and we initiate projects. We try to do things well, to honor God with our relationships and contribute to kingdom expansion. But these issues become problematic when you misuse relationships or accomplishments to satisfy your deep needs for security, acceptance, and personal worth. All those issues are rightly satisfied in only one relationship—your relationship with Jesus. Your relationship with him must be your ultimate satisfaction. Every other relationship and every other source of success is like a sugar high. The buzz feels good for a while but leaves you deflated in the end.

One woman became a Christian at the age of fifteen and met a young man her same age two weeks later. They became a couple and stayed together for about five years. They had a God-honoring relationship—morally pure, spiritually focused, and ministry involved. She assumed she had found the love of her life. Unfortunately, she had—but not with the results she expected.

After her second year of college, her boyfriend ended their relationship and later married her best friend. She was deeply wounded. For a while, she also lost any semblance of her relationship with God. With help from her friends and pastor, she discovered she had made an honest but horrific mistake. She had allowed her relationship with God to be defined by her relationship with her boyfriend. Because he had come into her life so soon after her conversion, she had intermingled two important relationships—her boyfriend and Jesus.

In her defense, it was a natural mistake for a young woman to make. She assumed God had allowed her boyfriend to enter her life to help shape and grow her spiritually. Her assumption was correct. But, unfortunately she allowed her earthly relationship with him to define her spiritual relationship with God (rather than the other way around). When one was strong, the other was also sound. But when her boyfriend left her, so did her sense of a relationship with God. Her profound disappointment, resulting from misplaced affection, took years to overcome.

While women often set their affections on relationships, men often set their affections on accomplishments. Men are more likely to fixate on proving their worth through their work. One Christian professional baseball player labored in the minor leagues for ten years. He continually struggled emotionally, berating himself for not reaching the big leagues as rapidly as he assumed he would and as his friends were doing. He continually asked God to make him successful so he could play major league baseball. But, no matter how hard he tried, he simply couldn't get there. His failure was eating him alive.

Finally he was promoted to the big leagues. He was happy but not giddy when he told me the news. He said, "During this past off-season, God convicted me that baseball was my god. Baseball was more than a job. It was what made me a man. Playing well meant I felt good about myself; playing poorly meant I beat myself up. I repented. I put God first in my life. I prayed, 'If I never play in the big leagues, I'll be satisfied. You are my life, my happiness, not baseball.'" When he was promoted to the major leagues, he celebrated accomplishing a life goal. But he no longer allows baseball to define him personally. He has set his affections on "things above" and discovered the satisfaction of drawing fulfillment from his relationship with Jesus, not his accomplishments as an athlete. This was a difficult but necessary spiritual change for a man whose life has been defined by his baseball accomplishments since he was a boy. When everyone else values you only for your production, it is difficult to remember God simply values *you for who you are.*

Our Disappointments Equip Us to Comfort Others

When you have been through a difficult experience, it marks your soul in ways others can detect. We can say, "I know what you're going through" or "I know how you feel," and the person we are speaking to believes us. We sense unmistakable authenticity when someone has been through what we are experiencing, has really shared our pain. Paul described it this way, "Blessed be the God and Father of our Lord Jesus Christ, the Father of mercies and the God of all comfort. He comforts us in all our affliction, so that we may be able to comfort those who are in any kind of affliction, through the comfort we ourselves receive from God" (2 Cor. 1:3–4).

One of our most disappointing life experiences was going through two miscarriages. Though disappointing for me, they were devastating for my wife. Her first pregnancy had been routine (sounds just like a man!). She had no reason to anticipate having problems with her next two. Yet both ended in miscarriage. We struggled through dark nights, discouraged, with many unanswered questions.

A few years later we met a couple named Terry and Suzanne. They badly wanted a baby but struggled to get pregnant. Finally, the big news! A baby was on the way. After such a long wait and so many setbacks, they were elated. Imagine their disappointment a few weeks later when Suzanne had a miscarriage. They turned to us for help. We were able to say, "We've been there," and help them with their loss. We walked with them through a grief process and helped them regain their spiritual equilibrium.

Something profound happened through sharing this experience. They developed a deep bond with us, and through us, a more profound confidence in God. A few months later Suzanne was pregnant again. We shared their tension of trying to limit expectations while at the same time being excited about the coming baby. We were all relieved when the baby reached full term, healthy in every way and ready to come into the world.

Then, a frantic phone call! Suzanne was in labor, it wasn't going well, and Terry wanted me to come immediately. I raced to the hospital and found Terry pacing in the hallway. "Good," he said, "you're here and Suzanne needs you," as he dragged me into the delivery room.

Chaos! The doctor was working hard, nurses scurrying, and blood everywhere. Terry held Suzanne's right hand and told me to take her other hand and pray. I did. I held on, literally, until the baby came. Thanks to a great doctor and God's protection, a bouncing baby boy entered the world. One year later, and on his birthday for the next seventeen years, Suzanne sent us a picture of her son and thanked us for our ministry to her during his birth. God used us to help this couple, to comfort them, and then support them, because we shared a common painful experience. God gave us entrée for continued life impact over the years because of the bonding made possible by our miscarriages.

Sometimes God allows us to experience pain so we can help others with similar problems. An aura of authenticity, created by the scars on our souls, connects us with the deepest hurts of others. There is no shortcut to being equipped to offer genuine comfort to hurting people. Wounded people give the best comfort.

Our Disappointments Guide Us to Better Options

When we pursue a plan of action, all along believing we are pursuing God's plan, it's disappointing to have poor results. One of my favorite biblical passages is the travel summary of Paul's missionary team in Acts 16:6–8: "They went through the region of Phrygia and Galatia and were prevented by the Holy Spirit from speaking the message in the province of Asia. When they came to Mysia, they tried to go into Bithynia, but the Spirit of Jesus did not allow them. So, bypassing Mysia, they came down to Troas." That was weeks and weeks of walking!

The phrases interpreting God's direction are very interesting. The team was "prevented by the Holy Spirit from speaking" in Asia. Why? Surely God wanted the people in that province to hear the gospel. And how did the Spirit prevent them from speaking? Governmental opposition, community disinterest, laryngitis? The Spirit of Jesus then kept the team from entering Bithynia. Again, why? And how were they prevented from entering? Finally they arrived in Troas where Paul had his vision of going to Macedonia—where God apparently wanted the team all along.

While there are many questions, and few specific answers about how it all happened, it's evident this team wandered across a large area seeking opportunities for gospel ministry. That's so encouraging! Often we assume everyone in the Bible knew exactly what to do, where to go, and how to proceed. Not so. Sometimes, just like leaders today, biblical leaders wandered around doing the best they could, trying to find God's will. God allowed Paul's missionary team to be turned away, to waste effort looking into fruitless opportunities, and to wander a winding path to the right conclusion. Sometimes disappointment closes doors so God can get us to go another direction.

This has happened repeatedly to me in personnel selection. Part of leading is selecting staff, and in my current role, faculty. Occasionally I have settled on someone I really wanted on my team, only to be thwarted for one reason or another. But in almost every case, within a very short time it became evident God had prevented me from hiring the wrong person. While writing this chapter, it happened again. We were searching for a new faculty member and had identified an acceptable candidate. We went through the full process and then he decided, at the last minute, not to join us. I was disappointed! But within a week, a new candidate emerged who was a much better fit than the previous one. Once again, we spent months on a disappointing process—only to have God give us a nudge in a better direction.

A friend had the same experience on a pastor search committee. The committee worked for months, narrowing a list of more than one hundred candidates to one. When the committee took its final vote, it was deadlocked—half yes and half no. Discouraging! The committee had to start over. But within two months, a new candidate emerged who became the committee's unanimous choice. The church affirmed the nomination with a 98 percent vote. Months later my friend wrote, "Every Sunday as I listen to the preaching and look around the contented congregation, I understand God led us through disappointment to his exact man for our church." In mysterious ways, God sometimes allows us to come to the end of ourselves, our searches, our plans—and then we are ready to receive his direction.

Our Disappointments Create Longing for Heaven

Life now, even on its best days, is far from perfect. Yet we sometimes expect life to be heavenly. It isn't. Life is disappointing. Not *can be* disappointing, but *is* disappointing. We err when we expect life to be fully satisfying, to be fulfilling. While we shouldn't be doomsayers or negative whiners, we have to be realistic. Life now is far from perfect.

But a better day is coming. God has given us "an inheritance that is imperishable, uncorrupted, and unfading, kept in heaven for you. . . . You rejoice in this, though now for a short time you have had to be distressed by various trials" (1 Pet. 1:4, 6). Have you noticed how little contemporary Christian music is about longing for heaven? That's an observation, not a criticism. One exception is the popular song "I Can Only Imagine." A friend has a sister with a debilitating illness. He wrote me, "My sister's 'hell' of just lying there, still mentally alert but totally incapable of moving—depending on others for everything—has given new meaning to lyrics of songs. She can't make it through 'I Can Only Imagine' without the kind of deep sobbing that just rips your heart to the core." Our disappointments remind us how broken, perverted, and unfulfilling this world is—and how sweet heaven will be someday. Life's most profound disappointments create a deep longing for heaven.

Conclusion

Leaders who make good choices and passionately pursue God will still be disappointed. People and projects will let you down. Don't despair! You're in good company among generations of Christian leaders. God is at work in all circumstances to accomplish good. Through disappointment you can share the sufferings of Jesus, redirect your affections, comfort others, find new direction, and refocus on the hope of heaven. Being disappointed may be a pathway to spiritual growth you didn't expect. Disappointment keeps us from loving this world too much and helps us focus on Jesus—our eternal and present hope.

This chapter has been about circumstances you can't control, about situations that sour despite your best efforts. Now we turn to another kind of painful circumstances for which you are responsible. Sometimes painful circumstances are your fault. They are caused by your bad decisions or sinful choices (or a double-barreled combination of both). Let's shift our focus in the next chapter to handling mistakes—problems you cause and their consequences.

4

Resolving Your Mistakes

Disappointment results from unfulfilled expectations. When you do your best and things just don't work out as you hoped, you experience the expectation gap and feel disappointed. Disappointment happens when you do your best, follow God's plan as you understand it, and have less-than-stellar outcomes. You learn from or manage the results, but they aren't always your responsibility or under your control. We focused on those situations in the last chapter.

But what happens when you *are* responsible? Responding in those situations is another matter entirely. Leaders *cause* painful situations by bad decisions or sinful choices. Sometimes a decision is one or the other—oftentimes a little bit of both. Both bad decisions and sinful choices, depending on the scope of the decision, can have wide-ranging consequences. On lesser issues, leaders can often recover quickly by admitting their mistakes, changing course, and moving in new directions. But other times, our bad decisions and sinful choices can have devastating results.

One friend who learned I was writing this book sent this note: "Someone ought to write a book on the painful side of leadership for the people in the pews. The cost to churches and God's kingdom because of the moral, financial, relational, and ego failures of church leaders is huge—and in large churches makes headlines in the secular media. I realize leaders suffer a great deal of injury because of what their followers do and say, but God's Word speaks far more to the cost of failed leaders: false prophets, evil kings, and money-grubbing, power-hungry priests. The blind leaders of the blind caught the bulk of Christ's condemnation."

Ouch! But his point is well taken. The biblical condemnations of leaders who misuse authority and abuse followers are potent (for example, Jesus's blistering rebuke of the scribes and Pharisees in Matt. 23). When we consider the high cost of bad leadership decisions, we understand the importance of heeding those warnings.

Another friend was a successful businessman with an executive position in a large corporation, plus a rental property company he privately owned. He had three teenage sons. He was an active deacon in a large church and chairman of the church's personnel committee. He and his wife built their lives around their family and their church. In short, he was the kind of competent leader a pastor depends on to build a strong church.

One night he was summoned to a special meeting of the personnel committee in which he learned the youth pastor had been caught in an adulterous relationship with a church member. The sordid details were shared with the committee.

A strategy to dismiss the offender, inform the church, manage the legalities, and handle the fallout within the membership was outlined and discussed. The committee was shocked but somehow stumbled through the process of making a plan to move forward.

My friend left the meeting to drive home. As the full impact of what had happened settled into his soul—he felt sick. More than feeling sick, he was sick. He pulled over, opened his car door, and vomited in the street. That's the impact of serious leadership mistakes on loyal followers.

This horrible decision by a church leader turned the stomach of a dedicated layman, even an executive accustomed to managing significant stress on a daily basis. Bad leadership decisions damage our followers. Sinful choices can be devastating. The youth pastor in this situation created a painful leadership situation for himself, his family, his mistress, her family, and their church family. Whatever consequences he experienced, he deserved. God meant every word of his warning when he had Paul write, "God is not mocked. For whatever a man sows he will also reap, because the one who sows to his flesh will reap corruption from the flesh" (Gal. 6:7–8).

Leadership mistakes—both bad decisions and sinful choices—hurt followers. When a leader makes a mistake, what should he or she do? Is it possible to recover from a mistake? Can wounds be healed, trust restored, relationships mended, and effective leadership once again given when a leader has made a significant mistake? Are there "fatal mistakes" that disqualify a leader from continuing in leadership?

While every situation requires a unique response based on the circumstances, there are key principles and practices leaders can follow to properly handle their mistakes. Let's consider both kinds of leadership mistakes—what happens when you make a bad decision and what happens when you make a sinful choice (and sometimes the intermingled combination of the two)—as we discover how to resolve leadership mistakes.

Take Responsibility for Your Actions

"Take responsibility for your actions" sounds too basic, like something a first-grade teacher would say to a student caught cheating on an exam. Accepting personal responsibility is a simple life lesson children are taught from the time they are able to make independent choices. Yet, despite early tutoring, we all seem to struggle perpetually with the problem of personal responsibility. Christian leaders aren't exempt. We struggle to take responsibility for our actions—especially when they have painful consequences.

The devil likes to whisper, "Pass the buck" or "Let someone else take the fall" or "You're the victim here!" Sometime ago I damaged a rental car on the first morning of a weeklong rental. Over that week I was frequently tempted to find a way to get out of admitting I was negligent. Every day some reason for avoiding admitting fault would pop into my head. At first I entertained those options. But once I determined to take responsibility, the devilish thoughts became almost amusing. After my decision was made, when thoughts of lying about the accident came to mind, I would pray silently, "Nice try, Satan, but you'll have to do better than that."

I returned the car, filed an honest claim, and took responsibility for my actions. But then another more troublesome temptation arose a few weeks later. Another car I rented was damaged in a hotel parking lot by someone who didn't leave a note or acknowledge what he or she had done. I was angry. Why should I have to pay for this damage? It wasn't my fault. While that was true, it had happened on my watch. Rental contracts are clear—what happens while you have a car is your responsibility. The temptation was greater this time than it had been a few weeks before. But it wasn't my fault! There had to be a way out of paying for it. No way should my insurance rates take another hit because of someone else's irresponsibility.

Yet once again, I returned the car, pointed out the damage, and took responsibility for the repairs. This time, however, it wasn't amusing. It was a genuine struggle to do the right thing. Paying that money was a bitter pill to swallow.

These might seem like trivial illustrations, and in some sense, they are. But they illustrate the subtle temptation every leader faces to shirk responsibility. Most major leadership failures only appear to be cataclysmic. In reality, the climactic implosion is almost always the final step in a series of smaller decisions to shirk responsibility, shift blame, and believe the lie: "the rules just don't apply to me." Once you shirk a minor responsibility, it desensitizes you for the next temptation. Over time your spiritual senses are dulled and it becomes easier and easier to blame others for your actions.

Blaming others is a surefire recipe for lost leadership effectiveness (in the least) or lost leadership opportunity (at the worst). A few years ago two ministers—in separate incidents—were guilty of moral failure. The responses of the two ministers were diametrically opposite. One came forward and took full responsibility for his actions, blamed no one else, offered an immediate resignation, and asked for nothing from his church. He cooperated fully in making a public disclosure by reading a statement approved by the church leadership team without adding to or detracting from what he had agreed to say.

When the other man's actions were uncovered, he blamed his wife for his sins, stonewalled the resignation process, created a gossip back draft to undermine the church leaders who confronted him, and threatened legal action if he was terminated. He refused to make a public statement about his departure from his leadership role and opposed those who rightfully confronted him and removed him from his position. His marriage ultimately failed and his leadership role was lost.

Because the first man took full responsibility for his actions and demonstrated humility through the resignation process, his church responded with significant support for him and his family. They paid for him and his wife to go to an intensive marriage counseling retreat center. They also continued his salary and benefits for several months to assist his transition. The church insisted he remain a member and surrounded him and his wife with accountability partners to support them while they healed. Today that former minister is a committed lay leader in the same church. His marriage is intact and healthy.

After observing these two situations for several years, it's apparent one key decision defined these very different outcomes. The first minister admitted his mistake and took full responsibility for his actions. The second did neither. This was the predominant determining factor in how their followers responded to them and in the ultimate resolution of each situation.

Whether you have made a bad leadership decision or a sinful choice as a leader, the first step to rectifying the situation is taking full responsibility for your actions. If you did it, own up to it. Don't do some kind of creative, two-step shuffle trying to deflect blame. Take responsibility for your mistakes.

And, extending this a bit, take responsibility for what happens on your watch. One fellow has this magnetic sign on his truck: "Every day in the Navy was like Sunday on the farm." It's clear he loved his time in the Navy! When asked why, he said, "The discipline. I grew up wild, thinking I was a real tough guy. The Navy taught me to take responsibility and showed me how a strong man really acts. In the Navy, you take responsibility for what you do and for what happens on your watch."

On your watch. Good leaders take responsibility for their actions and for things that happen on their watch. This is countercultural today; in our litigious society people blame others for every mistake or problem. People treat their attorneys like sidearms and draw them at the slightest provocation. Real leaders take responsibility for their actions, resisting the temptation to shift blame to others. By doing so, anger is diffused and forgiveness and restoration become possible.

Admit You Were Wrong

Taking responsibility for your actions is foundational. "I did it" must be your simple admission. The next step follows naturally from the first. After owning up to what you have done, admit you were wrong (in the case of a bad decision). This may also include confessing sin (when your mistake was also a sinful choice). Confessing your sin to God may be sufficient. But sometimes it isn't. For leaders, public confrontation (like Paul confronting Peter in Gal. 2:11–14) and public confession (Peter admitting prejudice and changing his convictions in Acts 11:4–18) may be required to repair a damaging situation. This doesn't mean you have to tell everyone, each and every one of your sins or shortcomings. But it does mean you sometimes confess to an appropriate circle of people impacted by your actions that you have been wrong, have sinned, or have changed your mind on a significant issue.

Taking responsibility means you say, "I did it." That's hard enough. It's often even harder to add, "I was wrong" and even more challenging to conclude, "And I sinned." This is the progression of admitting you were wrong. Take responsibility for your bad decisions. Admit fault. And, in the case of sinful choice, add, "And I sinned."

Are you old enough to remember the television show *Happy Days*? Set in the 1950s, the iconic character Fonzie was a macho stud whom men feared and women adored. He was cool—always right, always so smooth. But in one episode, he made a serious mistake. When confronted by his friends, he was forced to admit, "I was wrong." Only he couldn't say the words. It came out, "I was wrrrrrrrrrr." He tried and tried to speak the word *wrong*, but it just wouldn't come out of his mouth! Preserving his image made it impossible to admit his mistake.

Too many leaders are like this. We are excessively image conscious. We want our followers to believe we are always right, always in control, always accurate in our judgments and decisions. We are often driven by insecurities to present a façade of competence. Our very human selves simply can't be displayed lest we lose the loyalty, respect, and trust of our followers. Getting past all this and learning to take responsibility and admit wrongdoing is, however, essential for developing authentic leadership relationships.

If "I love you" are the three most important words in a romantic relationship, "I was wrong" may be the three most important words in establishing leadership credibility. When you make a mistake, your credibility helps your followers tolerate your behavior until you come to your senses. Frankly, your followers know you aren't always right. They see your shortcomings. They live with your bad decisions. They put up with your mistakes. The issue isn't *if* you will make mistakes. The issue isn't *if* your followers will observe those mistakes. The fundamental issue is: will you be transparent and humble enough to admit flaws, handle the consequences, and still continue to lead?

What kind of bad decisions do leaders make? Here are a few from my hall of shame. Back in the 1980s I felt our small church should have a television ministry. Under my leadership, we spent several months trying to make it happen. Dumb, dumb, dumb! My leadership team was against the idea from the beginning but went along out of loyalty to my self-labeled "innovative, faith-filled" dream. Fortunately I came to my senses before we spent too much time and money on that folly.

Another time I insisted our organization adopt a budget larger than recommended by our financial planners. Why? We had to have faith! We had to be bold and trust God to provide! Yes, my leadership team agreed, but we also had to make prudent plans based on our collective wisdom and experience. We adopted the larger budget and two months into the fiscal year were making cutbacks and revisions. Another stellar leadership decision on my part! These mistakes, bad leadership decisions, were relatively easy to overcome. Some aren't so easily resolved.

One of my worst leadership mistakes was using a long-range planning team to manipulate a church decision-making process. Rather than confront a flawed organization and ineffective people in their leadership roles, I attempted an "end run" to circumvent existing structures. The result was the worst church meeting I ever attended. People reacted angrily, yelled at each other, some left the meeting in tears, and in the end my plans (and the church's fellowship) were in shambles. At first the temptation was to blame others. But after a few months I admitted what I had done and started the recovery process. This example leads to the second aspect of admitting a mistake.

Sometimes admitting a bad decision also involves confessing sin. Not every bad leadership decision is necessarily sinful. But many are at least tainted with sin—ego was the root of my proposed television ministry, and pride influenced the bad budget decision. Others are just sin—pride, arrogance, greed, self-promotion—masquerading in some holier-than-thou leadership mantle. In the case of the failed long-range planning process, I had to confess the sin of using people to further my agenda. There is a fine but very definite line between working through people and working people to get what you want. I was miles past the line.

This kind of leadership mistake can only be overcome by

admitting the decision was wrong and confessing the sin that motivated it. Confession is a private matter, but for leaders it can also be a public responsibility. Part of taking a spiritual leadership role is assuming public responsibility for your actions. That is why novices shouldn't be rushed into spiritual leadership. The public responsibility of leadership can be excruciatingly painful (for the leader and the followers) when a leader sins and must confess sin to his followers.

Repairing this kind of leadership breach means a leader admits, "I was wrong and I sinned in the process." Public confession need not be more specific than necessary. In my case mentioned above, it involved admitting to misusing the process and asking the church to forgive me. I did this in a public worship service, after having made the same confession privately to the church's deacons. After making my public statement, the deacon chairman affirmed my leadership on behalf of the deacons and encouraged the church to do the same. Many people talked with me after my confession. Some confessed their sinful actions as well. While the entire problem was not resolved nor every hurt feeling soothed, we made substantial progress through the simple Christian acts of confessing sin and receiving forgiveness.

The Bible promises, "If we confess our sins, He is faithful and righteous to forgive us our sins and to cleanse us from all unrighteousness" (1 John 1:9). Most leaders use this verse liberally to help followers deal with their sin. The same promise is also true for leaders. When we confess our sins, God forgives them. James adds, "Confess your sins to one another and pray for one another, so that you may be healed" (James 5:16). While that verse's context is praying for physical healing, the principle has broader application. There are times, particularly for leaders who make decisions with broad impact, when public confession of sin is necessary to restore fellowship with other believers and credibility with the larger community. Public confession, when required, should take place in the spirit of Galatians 6:1–2,

> Brothers, if someone is caught in any wrong-doing, you who are spiritual should restore such a person with a gentle spirit, watching out for yourselves so you won't be tempted also. Carry one another's burdens; in this way you will fulfill the law of Christ.

When public confession is required, keep these principles in mind. First, confess your sin without including others. You are confessing *your* sin, not the sins of others. For example, when a pastor confessed to misusing church funds, he did not include the names of persons he spent the money entertaining. Second, confess the sin only in the scope it was committed. If your sin impacted a class or choir, confess it to them—not the church. If it only impacted two or three team members, confess it personally—not in a staff meeting. Third, confess the sin as personally as possible. Do it in person if possible. Make a phone call if you can't meet in person. Write a letter or publish your statement only if that's the only way to connect with your constituency.

Public confession may not be a common event for a leader, but it's an important spiritual discipline for repairing spiritual damage and relational trust. When you say, "I am wrong" and "I sinned," the vast majority of people will forgive you and continue to support you as a leader. The number of American politicians who have remained in office after seemingly superficial confessions of immoral actions illustrates the lengths most people will stretch to find a way to forgive their leaders. While that's a bad model for the church, it does illustrate how much people want their leaders to stay in place and how willing they are to forgive them if they take responsibility for their actions. Genuine confession, coupled with repentance, leading to forgiveness and restoration is the purview of the Christian community. We should model it genuinely, effectively, and powerfully—and much more frequently.

Accept the Consequences

Only in sappy movies and fairy tales does everyone live happily ever after with complete resolution of every difficulty. Leadership mistakes always have consequences. Sometimes those consequences result in termination from a specific leadership position or disqualification from any future leadership role. But most mistakes can be overcome and negative consequences managed. Leadership change in any organization is difficult, and most people want to help their leaders remain in place and succeed. But still, when you make a mistake, you have to live with the consequences.

What kind of consequences should be expected? Public embarrassment may be part of this process. Pain results from being exposed, from having the ugly side of your motives and actions revealed. Loss of stature is a related consequence. Your leadership influence may be diminished because of your mistake. Followers can be emotionally deflated, not quite so willing to support your next decision or initiative. Some bad decisions are costly. Your ministry may reallocate money to recover from the bad decision and donors may stop or diminish their support. You may also suffer personal financial setbacks—loss of compensation while the ministry recovers, money you may contribute to offset ministry loses, and restitution you may need to pay.

You can mitigate the pain by taking several steps. First, accept the consequences as a normal part of the recovery process. It isn't easy to admit you made a mistake, confess your sins, refocus, and lead your church or organization in another direction. Trust has been damaged, credibility undermined, and momentum lost. Nothing you can do will make all this magically disappear.

Second, trust God to restore your leadership. God limits damage from painful circumstances and delights in restoring repentant leaders. While we aren't sure of all the reasons, Mark was demoted as a young leader and dismissed from Paul's missionary team (Acts 15:38–39). Later, however, Mark was restored to a leadership role (2 Tim. 4:11) and wrote a gospel. Whatever mistakes he made as a young leader were overcome by God's grace and his continued record of effective leadership.

Third, allow time for healing to take place. Wounds heal but not instantly. Scabs form and fall away, but scars remain. Over time scars fade but remain memory marks of significant past events. I am a cancer survivor. My scars remain but are much less prominent than a decade ago. Seeing them still reminds me of a life crisis through which God worked powerfully. Leadership scars aren't as visible but are nonetheless real. They remind us of past events, what we learned through the pain, and how God sustained us. Allow time for healing, realizing the resulting scars will be permanent assets in your leadership experiences portfolio. My leadership scars, not my successes, are the source for much of the material in this book and are often my most compelling life message.

Move On

For many, the most perplexing part of a bad leadership decision or a sinful choice is how to put it behind them and move on. When you take responsibility—admit you were wrong, confess your sin, and receive forgiveness—you should be finished with the issue. While you must live with the consequences, the actual events have been addressed and resolved. It's time to move on.

This is difficult because leaders, like everyone else, have a built-in ability to remember every mistake and perpetually replay it in their minds. TiVo has nothing on the human brain! We have an incredible capacity to mentally record all our stupid, embarrassing, or otherwise humiliating actions and recall them (and how they made us feel) at a moment's notice. One young leader made the common mistake—overpromise, under-deliver. When she didn't fulfill her promise, many were disappointed. She did the right thing. She admitted what she had done and asked for forgiveness, and it was granted. She told a friend, "I learned a big-time lesson on that one!" But that wasn't the end of it. Day after day, it was on her mind and in frequent conversations with friends. While she had dealt with the issue, she continued to rehash it mentally, berating herself for her mistake. Moving on was tough.

Bigger mistakes take longer to recover from emotionally and longer to put in the past. But put them in the past we must! Reliving past mistakes cripples future initiative. Leaders must learn the discipline of *failing fast.* When you make a mistake, own up to it and move on—quickly. Don't gloss over it, but don't dwell on it either. Moving on means you stop talking about the mistake (except as a "learning moment" that guides future decisions), release yourself from false guilt, and take the initiative to head in more healthy directions. Moving on requires spiritual and emotional discipline. Take charge of your negative emotions and move on.

A chief problem at this point is your inability to forgive yourself. Some leaders say, "I know God has forgiven me, but I just can't forgive myself." That sounds so spiritual. In reality, it's veiled arrogance. How can you place your judgment about your sin above God's judgment? God forgives confessed sin. He commands his people to do the same. And yet you claim a higher standard, the inability to forgive yourself? Come down off your spiritual high horse! No sin is too great for God's forgiveness. Your standards shouldn't be higher than his. When God forgives, you are forgiven. Case closed. Move on.

Fatal Mistakes

Are there some mistakes that are fatal to your leadership role or identity? Yes, but not as common as you might assume. Most mistakes can be overcome, most sins forgiven and put behind you. There are a few mistakes (or cumulative sets of mistakes) and a few sinful choices with consequences so great you simply can't overcome them and lead effectively in your current setting (or in rare cases, ever again in any setting). For example, one administrator made a series of bad decisions in selecting leaders for his organization. Gradually people lost confidence in his wisdom. His bad decisions were well-intentioned but led to organizational ineffectiveness. He learned from his mistakes but eventually needed a fresh start in another setting. He avoided making the same mistakes again and continues to provide effective leadership in a new position.

Another leader, however, lost both his leadership role and identity because of sinful choices. He lost the privilege of Christian leadership because of immoral and illegal sexual contact with a teenager, resulting in his imprisonment. This person made a sinful choice with such devastating consequences as to permanently lose the trust of the Christian community. He was later forgiven and restored to Christian fellowship but not to Christian leadership. Some sins so violate relational trust that the opportunity to continue in a formal leadership role is forever forfeited.

Conclusion

You can overcome leadership mistakes—bad decisions and sinful choices. Take responsibility for your actions. Admit when you are wrong. Confess your sins—to God and publicly to your followers when necessary. Then move on.

As you read this, you may be thinking, "That isn't so new. That's simply the biblical prescription for such problems applied to leaders." Exactly! In some ways, this is Discipleship 101 applied to leadership. The problem for some leaders is the process seems too simple. For others, we doubt the same process works for followers *and leaders*. Our sins just seem too big, too troublesome, with too many negative consequences.

This process is simple but profound. It works for everyone—including leaders. So use these steps—take responsibility, admit when you are wrong, confess your sin, and move on. Doing so will liberate you from the debilitating problem of being stalemated by residual guilt and oppressive discouragement because of your mistakes as a leader.

God knows the frailty of your heart, your propensity for sin, and your weaknesses as a leader. He uses you anyway. Part of remaining useful is resolving your mistakes appropriately. God has given you the means to do this. Take advantage of his gracious provision. Don't be limited by past mistakes or bad decisions. Resolve them and move on!

When you make a serious mistake, repentance and recovery can be a lonely process. That isn't, however, the only occasion when leaders feel isolated and alone. Understanding the reasons for loneliness and how to cope with it is a pressing need for all leaders at one time or another. Let's turn our attention now to the problem of coping with loneliness.

5

Coping with Loneliness

"Chapter 1 in your book should be about loneliness," was one leader's advice about the severity of this problem. Loneliness is an occupational hazard of Christian leadership. Yet this seems paradoxical. Christian leaders work in Christian communities, fellowships of people committed to similar values, goals, and dreams. Christian leaders work in churches and organizations that value relationships. We share fellowship with other believers because of our shared relationship with God through Jesus. But, while we have the capacity for remarkable relational intimacy and depth, Christian leaders still experience loneliness.

Is loneliness really an occupational hazard of Christian leadership? Should we expect to be lonely? Or does loneliness indicate something is wrong with us? Are there reasons—positive and negative—for loneliness? If there are positive reasons, is there a purpose or reason why God allows us to be lonely? And if there are negative reasons, should we make lifestyle or leader-style adjustments to mitigate the problem? Were leaders in the Bible ever lonely? If so, what can we learn from their example? These are some of the questions to consider as we develop resources to cope with loneliness in leadership.

Why Are Christian Leaders Lonely?

Browsing in a bookstore several years ago, I came across a pamphlet on loneliness among leaders by Charles Swindoll titled *The Lonely Whine of the Top Dog*. While I have long since lost the booklet, the title was so intriguing it has stuck with me for many years. Being a "top dog" can be a lonely, isolating experience. Some reasons are inevitable—they simply come with the territory. When a person assumes a leadership role, the role itself makes the leader unique and separates him from his followers. Even in a team environment, where there is shared responsibility and community, the buck has to stop with someone. The finality of ultimate responsibility makes leadership a lonely experience. Let's consider some dimensions of leadership that create lonely leaders.

Leaders feel lonely because they are isolated by information.

Leaders know information about their followers they aren't able to share with anyone. The information can be personal—like a pastor knowing who has a drinking problem or who was abused as a child. Or the information can be more professional—like the negative results of a personnel evaluation. One of the ways this creates leadership isolation is through decisions regarding team members. When a person—paid or volunteer—is dismissed, demoted, removed from, or refused a leadership role, the leader who makes this decision usually can't reveal the reasons. It's a lonely feeling to have a former employee freely sharing her version of her termination story, while you remain silent. Some will side with the disgruntled person while assuming the worst about you. The temptation to break confidence and share the details of a decision is powerful. Yet doing so accomplishes no good purpose, other than to defend your reputation as a leader. As a leader, you can't be that self-serving.

It's equally painful when your decisions about followers, based on private information, are later second-guessed. For example, one pastor refused to allow a prominent church member to access church funds or otherwise supervise church finances. From the outside it appeared to be a power play by the pastor to keep an influential person from contesting his direction of church resources. The real reason, however, was different. The pastor, through counseling with the man's wife, knew he had a compulsive gambling problem and the family finances were in disarray. The pastor was unable to disclose this information and was accused of being unwilling to share leadership with a man others admired for his supposed financial acumen. He held his ground, but it was lonely ground to hold.

In another instance a pastor refused to perform a wedding for a couple when he discovered evidence of physical abuse in the relationship. He was unwilling to perform the wedding until this serious issue was adequately resolved. Of course, he wasn't able to share publicly the reasons for his decision. The bride-to-be, embarrassed by allowing herself to be victimized by her fiancé, publicly shared other dubious reasons for the pastor's reluctance. When church members reacted negatively to his decision, not performing the wedding was a lonely position to maintain.

Information, and the need to maintain confidentiality, isolates leaders. We know facts about people in our organization that inform our decisions about them. Yet we are often not at liberty to disclose this information—even to support our decisions or defend ourselves from scurrilous attacks. When you become a leader, you gain access to information you wouldn't otherwise have. You also assume responsibility to handle that information appropriately, even when doing so is painful.

Leaders feel lonely because they are isolated by obedience.

Obeying God can be a lonely experience—consider Jeremiah, Isaiah, John the Baptist, or a host of other biblical characters. Like those men and women who obeyed God and found themselves isolated by their choices, leaders today have the same experience. In some places in the world, Christian leaders are arrested, imprisoned, and tortured for their obedience to God. Their passion for kingdom expansion is perceived as a threat to the state or national religion, and they suffer consequences. One such leader experienced years of loneliness, imprisoned with very limited opportunity to be visited by family members. It was unsafe for church members or other friends to be associated with him while he was a prisoner. His experience closely paralleled biblical characters who truly suffered, alone, for their obedience to God.

For most leaders the isolation of obedience isn't this dramatic. It is, however, real in more subtle ways. For example, when a Christian leader takes a stand for a moral cause—like opposition to gay marriage or advocating justice for the poor—public ridicule often follows. In Western culture, the most egregious insult today is being called "intolerant." This is a code word describing anyone who articulates moral values based on absolute truth. In previous generations *tolerance* was defined as respecting persons who held a position with which you disagreed. Today *tolerance* has been redefined as accepting every belief as equally valid and affirming every person's version of truth. When a leader advocates any absolute position based on the Bible (from the exclusivity of Jesus as Lord to the dignity of life for every person), that leader will be called *intolerant*—almost a profanity in the twenty-first century!

Taking a moral stand is lonely, not only because of attacks from outsiders who disagree with a leader's position, but also because of a growing ambiguity in the Christian community about the nature of truth, the appropriateness of absolute standards, and the right position on moral issues. In short, beware of friendly fire. Taking a moral stand may be a lonely decision—and it may become even lonelier as moral absolutes are rejected more decisively in the future.

Leaders are also isolated by obedience in other ways. When a leader senses God's direction for his organization, he must be the first to make lifestyle adjustments to facilitate the change. A pastor who wants his church to build a new facility must be the first to make a financial commitment to the project. When the elders of a church are burdened to increase the spiritual devotion of their church's members, they first must fast, pray, and consecrate themselves before leading the church through a similar process. When a leader determines God is leading in a specific direction, the leader must obey God first—often long before anyone else joins the process. Leaders are often ahead of the curve of organizational obedience. They set the pace, often alone, through personal obedience to God so they can later lead their organization to corporate obedience. Obeying God in this way can be a lonely experience.

Leaders feel lonely because they are isolated by job demands.

Because leaders are public figures—making speeches, preaching sermons, chairing meetings, hosting receptions—it's often wrongly assumed public events occupy most of a leader's time. Most leaders spend a considerable amount of time alone. Doing their job effectively requires it.

Christian leaders spend time alone in prayer, Bible reading, and Bible study. Pastors, of course, are expected to do this. But all Christian leaders must maintain daily devotional practices, including Bible reading and study. And while group prayer and study are also helpful, there's no substitute for meeting God personally and privately. Maintaining this discipline means choosing to be alone for significant amounts of time on a regular basis.

Another isolating job requirement is studying problems, analyzing data, and creating proposals to move your organization forward. This takes time and requires a leader to be alone. Group thinking is essential in organizational leadership, but leaders must analyze problems privately as well as participate in group thinking. Very complex problems require many hours of private study, deliberation, and drafting proposed solutions. While ultimate decisions are often made collaboratively, every leader needs private time to think clearly through challenging issues and possible solutions in order to make the best contribution to a group process. Working alone can lead to feeling lonely.

For some leaders travel is also an isolating experience. Travel requires a leader to be away from family and community. The glamour of business travel wears off quickly as you navigate the complexities of air travel, hotels, rental cars, lost luggage, weather problems, and wild taxi rides. Travel, when it goes well, requires a leader to spend long hours alone. When it goes poorly—sickness, delays, and fruitless meetings—the loneliness is even more acute.

Leaders may also be isolated by their schedule or their work setting. Leaders are busy. Keeping your schedule free of unnecessary meetings and appointments also means you are keeping your schedule free of people. The more limited your availability, the less interaction you have with people. This is a necessary and sometimes difficult discipline for leaders, particularly gregarious leaders. While most Christian leaders enjoy being with their followers and have some kind of open-door policy to interact with them, they also know they will never accomplish their priority tasks if they are not judicious in setting limits on their availability.

A leader's work environment can also contribute to loneliness. Perhaps the work environment where space is at the greatest premium is a nuclear submarine. Yet even in that environment, space is reserved for the captain to live, work, and even eat alone. He has a private cabin, private bathroom, and private work area. Command requires isolation—for resting and working in private so public leadership can be most effective. Most Christian leaders have a private office. The greater your responsibility, typically the more isolated your work space. This is often helpful, even necessary, but also contributes to the sense of isolation and loneliness you may feel.

Leaders feel lonely because of emotional depletion from job performance.

Christian leaders pour their hearts and souls into their work. We do this because we believe God has called us to our task. We view our work through a spiritual lens, believing our work is an expression of commitment and worship. Christian leadership is spiritual work engaged in a spiritual battle with eternal consequences. We take our work seriously and expend ourselves for our followers and the progress of our church or organization. One pastor wrote, "There isn't a night I lay my head on the pillow without thinking about how to reach someone who needs the Lord, how to help a troubled marriage, how to better lead my team, or how to disciple someone in my church. Just the burden of being responsible for the spiritual lives of people is a cause of loneliness." Because of passionate focus and the perpetual burden of spiritual leadership, we can be emotionally depleted and vulnerable to depression, hopelessness, and loneliness.

Elijah is a biblical example of this downward spiral. He was a prophet with remarkable ability to discern

God's direction and access God's power. He predicted a drought (1 Kings 17:1–7), miraculously provided for a widow (vv. 8–16), and then raised the same woman's son from the dead (vv. 17–24). This was all a prelude to his confrontation with Ahab and the prophets of Baal on Mount Carmel where he called down the fire of God (1 Kings 18). When it was over, Jezebel confronted Elijah with this warning, "May the gods punish me and do so severely if I don't make your life like the life of one of them by this time tomorrow" (1 Kings 19:2).

Elijah, the powerful prophet who prayed down God's consuming fire on Mount Carmel, "became afraid and immediately ran for his life. When he came to Beer-sheba . . . he left his servant there, but he went on a day's journey into the wilderness. He sat down under a broom tree and prayed that he might die. He said, 'I have had enough! LORD, take my life, for I'm no better than my fathers'" (1 Kings 19:3–4).

The prayer "I've had enough!" is a succinct statement of how a lonely leader feels. Elijah was spiritually and emotionally depleted. He had faced spiritual battle after spiritual battle—predicting the weather, providing for the poor, raising the dead, confronting false gods. He had emptied himself spiritually and emotionally through service. Then, as he traveled, he left his servant behind and continued alone into the wilderness. This is a typical pattern leading to loneliness—working hard, expending spiritual energy, encountering overwhelming challenges, hearing mean-spirited critics, and separating from your supporters. All of this can result in a leader praying, as Elijah did, "that he might die."

Christian leadership is hard work. It's spiritually and emotionally exhausting. It requires constant diligence, sacrificial service, and pastoral compassion for people. Christian leaders have constant pressure to maximize their impact with limited financial resources. This often means fund-raising, a very difficult task for many leaders, is a constant pressure. And, in addition to all this, there's the ever-present reality of spiritual warfare. The devil, his demons, and the world system under his influence all conspire to limit the effectiveness of Christian leaders. Christian leadership, when done conscientiously, can leave you feeling empty, vulnerable, and convinced it would be better to die than continue another day. When you are depleted from expending yourself in your work, you will feel lonely. It's a natural result of giving yourself wholeheartedly to your calling.

What to Do When You Feel Lonely

Two key words come to mind when developing strategies for coping with loneliness—relationships and expectations. Let's consider the first area, relationships, in more detail since managing expectations was a major "backdrop" strategy discussed earlier (see chapter 2).

Loneliness can be countered by developing meaningful relationships and entrusting yourself to God and others in difficult times. The primary relationship for countering loneliness is your relationship with God. Developing depth in your relationship with God through spiritual disciplines is foundational. But resting in and drawing on the intimacy those disciplines facilitate are essential when confronting loneliness. Building interpersonal relationships is also vital to countering loneliness. Let's look at both strategies.

Cultivate your awareness of God's presence.

One of the simplest, yet most profound spiritual realities for Christian leaders is the affirmation "God is with me." Several psalms are known as Psalms of Lament because of their plaintive content and tone. Yet, despite how forlorn the author, he determined to find hope in his relationship with God. In Psalm 31:9–12, he wrote, "I am in distress; my eyes are worn out from angry sorrow . . . my life is consumed with grief . . . I am ridiculed by all my adversaries and even by my neighbors. I am an object of dread to my acquaintances; those who see me in the street run from me. I am forgotten." Now that's lonely! He was beleaguered—beaten down from crying, ridiculed by enemies and friends, and shunned by people in public. But then the affirmation: "But I trust in You, LORD; I say, 'You are my God'" (v. 14).

Another example is Psalm 88:4–5, 8–9: "I am like a man without strength, . . . I am like the slain lying in the grave, . . . You have distanced my friends from me; . . . My eyes are worn out from crying." Again, that's lonely! He felt dead inside—as emotionally dead as if already in a grave—with no friends around to help. Eyes worn out from crying, he still affirmed, "But I call to You for help, LORD" (v. 13).

Believers, including Christian leaders, have an even more intimate relationship with God than these psalmists. Through conversion, and the resulting indwelling of the Holy Spirit, we have an intimate, inner, constant relationship with God. No matter how lonely you feel, you are never alone. It's a biblical impossibility. God is always with you!

One of my favorite short prayers is, "Lord, here *we* go." This is my frequent prayer before speaking, before leading a meeting, or before entering a stressful leadership situation. This simple prayer reminds me that God is with me. I don't have to ask him to be with me—he is in me through my relationship with Jesus and the permanent indwelling presence of the Holy Spirit. God is with me all the time, in every circumstance and situation. So, while it's possible to be without human companionship, it's impossible to be truly alone. God is with you. Always. All the time. In every situation. In every circumstance. Immanuel is more than a word used at Christmas to describe Jesus' incarnation. Immanuel is an ever-present, power-packed, theologically rich concept with personal and practical application. God is with you. Immanuel. Count on it!

You cultivate your awareness of God's presence by consistent devotional practices coupled with the discipline to "pray constantly" or "without ceasing" (1 Thess. 5:17). When you read the Bible daily, pray daily, occasionally practice fasting or other forms of personal self-discipline, and memorize Scripture, your sense of God's presence will deepen. These private worship practices facilitate fresh encounters with God. They remind you to practice God's presence through frequent, short, silent prayers as part of your daily routine. The practice of maintaining this continuing prayer dialogue is a significant reminder of God's presence and a strong help in dissipating loneliness. When these disciplines wane, so does a sense of spiritual and emotional well-being. When your awareness of God's presence is high, it's very difficult to feel lonely no matter how isolating your circumstances.

Cultivate friendships to sustain you through low times.

The proliferation of electronic communication tools seems to have made cultivating friendships easier. That's an incorrect assumption. Many people today maintain hundreds of names on their "friends" list on various Web sites and e-mail portals. Keeping up with hundreds of people has become an obligation, almost an obsession, with many people today. Yet these connections are often superficial. As one young leader told me, "My relationships are a mile wide, and about a quarter inch deep." He has substituted quantity of contact for quality in relationships. Superficial acquaintances can't sustain you through lonely times as a leader. You need something more. You need real friends—people with whom you share mutual interests, mutual joys, mutual pain, and common life experiences.

One kind of friendship to cultivate is with *ministry peers.* These are people who do the same kind of work you do, sometimes in your church or organization, but other times in another setting. These are friends who face the same kind of challenges you do, know the same pressures, and deal with the same issues. They are brothers in arms, comrades in combat. These are friends who nod knowingly when you start telling them about your struggles because they have the same experiences. Ministry peers are great friends to have when you feel you are the only person who has ever faced a dilemma or problem. They remind you that you aren't alone. These friends can also help you see the humor, even gallows humor, in your situation. They can help you keep perspective, to see the larger picture of what you are going through.

Early church leaders worked in a teamlike environment. The disciples often traveled in a large group, deployed in smaller groups, and were sent out two by two. Seldom are they portrayed working alone. In Acts, Paul usually traveled with a missionary partner or team. Much of Acts is written by Luke using "we" to describe the collective efforts of early missionaries. In his plaintive last written words (2 Tim. 4:9–22), Paul wrote a short summary of his faithful friends and lamented coworkers who had abandoned him. He appealed for Timothy to come quickly for companionship during his imprisonment. Paul clearly enjoyed working with ministry partners and drew support and strength from them.

What keeps ministry leaders from developing these kinds of friendships today? One common problem is competition among Christian leaders. We are reluctant to admit we have problems, because we are subtly competing with each other. Another problem is lack of transparency. Our ego keeps us from revealing too much about our struggles. We don't want to appear vulnerable or weak. Another issue is arrogance. We want others to think we "have it all together," so we avoid sharing any hint of personal struggles. Our propensity toward independence, a "Lone Ranger" attitude, is also a problem. Pride is the root of all this fakery.

To overcome these tendencies, take the initiative to develop key friendships with ministry peers. Humble yourself. Take the risk of reaching out to potential friends among your peers. Doing so will give you real allies when the dark times come. And remember, even the Lone Ranger had a faithful friend. The Lone Ranger wasn't really a lone ranger!

Another kind of friendship to cultivate is with *everyday people*. Leaders need friends who aren't part of their organization, who know them in another context, and who relate to them only as friends. Many leaders find it easy to make acquaintances but hard to make friends as they become more enmeshed in the demands of their leadership role. Several of my trusted friendships are with people I have known for years, friendships first made during our formative adult years in school and early ministry. Those relationships have been sustained over time and distance because of the depth of our relationship and the commonality of our interests. Sustaining these friendships takes work—phone calls, occasional trips, and other efforts to stay connected. For example, our family vacationed with another family several times when our children were all younger. The husband was (and is) one of my best friends. Our wives were also good friends, and our families were compatible enough to make spending a week together a positive experience—even during our encounter with the bear.

We were in separate vehicles from our friends, our car following their van. They stopped and signaled us to look out our window at something. Since they were seated higher in their van, I hopped out of the car to stand and look over the bushes at what they were seeing. Just as I stood up, so did the bear about twenty feet from me on the other side of a hedge. Everyone but me needed a long break to recover from their laughter at me diving back into the car!

Actually the bear story illustrates one of the principles of building relationships with everyday people—people who don't share your leadership role or who aren't part of your organization. These friendships are built around common interests and shared experiences. They are solidified by going through things—good and bad things—together. True friendships are built through emotionally engaging common experiences—births, deaths, graduations, parties, illnesses, promotions, relocations, and so on. When you have lived through significant events (good and bad), with transparency and mutual vulnerability, deep bonds are formed.

Another kind of friend to help you counter loneliness is a *trusted confidant*. These are hard to find and harder to keep (my older confidants keep passing away). As a leader, there are some things you can't talk about with your peers or share with friends. Some issues are too sensitive. Yet these issues can also be the most isolating, the most burdensome to bear. To keep these problems from overwhelming you with a sense of isola- tion leading to loneliness, you need a trusted confidant.

Over the years there have been a few men who have served me this way (my "wise guys"). These relationships developed through my seeking input from them, asking their counsel on delicate issues, trusting them with some of my thorniest problems, and confessing some of my worst mis- takes. Sustaining these relationships has been a vital part of my emotional stability as a leader. If you don't have a cadre of wise men (or wise women for female leaders), how do you start building these relationships? Look for the wisest people you know who have more life experience and insight than you do. These may be former pastors, professors, supervisors, or colleagues. They may be friends in your church or com- munity. Look for two essential qualities, wisdom and discre- tion, and not so much for outward titles or position.

These three types of friends can help you when you are lonely. It's important to continually cultivate these rela- tionships, not just call on people when you have a crisis. Friendships are built over time around shared experiences and common interests. They can't be forced, but they can be cultivated. Like a garden, friendships must be planted, nurtured, and protected so they produce an appropriate harvest. If you are lonely because of a scarcity of meaningful friendships, you can change your situation. It will take time but you can initiate, nurture, and protect vital relationships until they become the kind of friendships that sustain you as a leader.

You may wonder why I haven't included your spouse as a primary source of comfort and strength. My exclusion doesn't diminish the potential support from this significant relationship (note the dedication page of this book). But hear this caution! Don't put too much pressure on your spouse to be your only source of emotional strength during leadership trials. Often, your leadership struggles are shared by your spouse, who also needs support from you and other friends. So, yes, depend on your spouse for emotional support, but both of you should develop other meaningful relationships as well. Your marriage will be stronger if your spouse is part of a larger team sustaining your emotional health.

Embracing Loneliness and Solitude

Leadership can be an isolating experience and leaders are often lonely. But is that always bad? The answer, surprisingly, is no. There are at least two very positive ways God uses isolating circumstances to benefit leaders.

Choosing Solitude

The first is when a leader chooses to be alone. There is a difference between loneliness and solitude. Loneliness is an emotional state that overtakes a leader and can occur in the midst of multitudes. Solitude, on the other hand, is a choice to step away from normal activity for special spiritual purposes. Solitude isn't really being alone. It's choosing to be alone with God.

As a leader, you need time alone with God. This can take several forms. You need regular time for Bible reading and prayer. You need time for Bible study and Scripture memory. You need time for meditation, reflection, and perhaps journaling your insights about God's Word or work. These are good solitude habits to establish.

Some leaders also find more extended periods of solitude helpful. One pastor takes time each summer to go away to a retreat center to study, pray, and plan his preaching ministry for the following year. An administrator takes a weekend early each year to isolate himself with God to pray through problems and opportunities his organization will face the following year. Choosing solitude renews spiritual passion and restores emotional equilibrium. Remember, being alone isn't the same as being lonely.

Learning from Loneliness

Some spiritual lessons can only be learned, and some spiritual battles fought, in the crucible of profound loneliness. When Jesus went to the Garden of Gethsemane to pray prior to his crucifixion, he asked Peter, James, and John to accompany him. Jesus wanted his closest companions with him during what he anticipated would be an enormous trial. No one wants to be alone at a time like that. But Peter, James, and John fell asleep despite Jesus' repeated pleas for support. Their slumber meant Jesus faced his dark night of the soul alone (Matt. 26:36–46).

I have been desperately lonely, passing through my own dark night of the soul. Through that experience God taught me a profound lesson about our relationship. A few years ago I had cancer. The treatment circumstances required two surgeries within five days. The first surgery and recovery were routine. The second, performed on an emergency basis, was an ordeal.

After the second surgery, control of bodily functions returned very slowly. There were some complications that limited my recovery and threatened my long-term health. Because the second surgery was late in the day, my recovery took place in the evening and throughout the following night. It was an agonizing, seemingly endless night.

Unable to relax, but also largely unable to move, my muddled mind wished for only one thing—sleep! I would drift out of pain into sleep, then awaken, hoping for time to have passed only to see the clock had advanced only two or three minutes. This went on for hours. The only verse I could remember, really only a paraphrase, was "weeping lasts for the night, but joy comes in the morning" (see Ps. 30:5). My silent prayer was, "Lord, just get me through to morning." While my wife, Ann, stayed with me, there really wasn't much anyone could do to alleviate my situation. Like no other time in my life, I felt completely alone. My awareness to pray, even the one sentence "Lord, get me through to morning," was more spiritual reflex than an act of devotion. It was a result of practicing the presence of the Lord (as described earlier in the chapter) for many years. Thinking that prayer was all I could do.

During that long night, no external supports, relationships, or accomplishments made any difference to my spiritual or emotional well-being. Neither the degrees I had earned, the ministries I had led, the people I had influenced, the friendships I had cultivated, nor our money in the bank made any difference. I was undone, unable to help myself or be helped by anyone. When morning finally dawned, so did this spiritual reality. For the first time, my life had been reduced to God and me—and he was enough. He was enough! His sustaining presence was all I had—I couldn't even say a good prayer—and he was enough.

That night, recovering from my second surgery, was graduate school in understanding God's presence and trusting his sustaining power. Since that night I have faced many lonely leadership situations. During those trials my sustaining reality has been, "Lord, you are with me and I know that's enough." My capacity to lead through lonely, isolating circumstances was exponentially increased by my experience with God in that hospital room. Lonely times are essential. God teaches us lessons we can learn only through those circumstances. Thank God for lonely times, for trips through the desert alone, when the lessons learned become the foundation for future spiritual power.

Conclusion

As a leader, you will be lonely and sometimes alone. But a lot of the time, you will also be very much in the spotlight. Leadership, by its nature or definition can't be done without engaging people in relationships. In varying degrees this makes every leader a public figure—doing your work with people and in front of people. Let's shift our focus in the next chapter to the opposite extreme from the dark night of the soul—the bright spotlight of living your life in public and the challenges that brings.

6

Living in the
Spotlight

One of my favorite childhood games was Spotlight—hide-and-go-seek with flashlights. On warm summer nights the kids in my neighborhood would run around in the dark trying to "tag" each other with the beams from flashlights. We had variations of the game with bases, safety zones, flags to capture, and whatever else we could imagine to spice up the fun.

Leaders wish life in the spotlight was this much fun. Leaders live on stage in the spotlight of public observation and opinion. Part of learning to lead is accepting leadership as a public role and learning to manage the consequences. From a distance the leadership spotlight looks inviting to the uninitiated. But leaders soon learn the spotlight is like a siren song—inviting from a distance, often painful to experience.

While most leaders expect their professional lives to be well known, the surprising discovery for many is how much their personal lives are considered public information, open for analysis by their followers. It's also surprising how supposedly private matters, like medical information, become public concerns. Leaders in churches or ministry organizations soon realize their lives are an open book read by all and reviewed by many. Some of the situations are common, others almost comical.

When you buy a new car, be ready for questions. Followers will ask how much you paid and imply they are overpaying you since you can afford such a luxury. Change your hair style or dress more casually, and you will be asked if you are having a midlife crisis. Announce you are going on vacation, and someone will ask where you are going, flying or driving, how long you will be gone, etc. Try to slip away without telling anyone your plans, and the rumor mill will insist you are looking for another job.

Leaders who are parents have many issues to deal with. Announcing a pregnancy or adoption can be interesting. One pastor told me a church member replied to his and his wife's announcement of their pending adoption, "That's great news. That's how all pastors should get their children." As opposed to the *other* way, I suppose! And after children arrive, parenting in public is a continuing challenge. Appropriate care for infants, choices about preschool programs, and discipline methods for children are all fodder for discussion. Decisions about education—homeschool, private school, Christian school, or public school—guarantee contrary opinions no matter the choice. As children turn into teenagers, as in every family, questions about church involvement must be decided in a leader's family. The difference for leaders is their decisions are openly evaluated and critiqued, making the already challenging time of adolescence even more difficult.

When a leader has a serious illness (or even a cold), it seems everyone wants to know the diagnosis and share an experience when an uncle, grandmother, or friend had the same problem. This is encouraging, on one level, as you appreciate the concern and attempts to express love for you. But it can quickly become uncomfortable or embarrassing when a health problem is more personal. Several years ago, Kansas City Royals team leader George Brett had to miss part of a World Series because of, as widely reported in the media, hemorrhoids. That's too much information! Nonetheless, a leader can expect even intimate health details to be discussed openly.

Grieving a loss is another life event made more difficult because it's done in public. Leaders, like their followers, experience profound loss. Leaders must deal with aging parents and, eventually, their deaths. Leaders also have friends and family who die—as well as other less dramatic grief-inducing losses like friends relocating, spouses losing jobs, or adult children going through difficult times in their careers or relationships. Sometimes you would really like to keep these issues private. But often your grief plays out in public, adding another dimension to it because you are a leader.

And then there's a leader's job, which is, by nature, a public responsibility. A leader lives *out loud*, personally and professionally. The pressure of always being *on*, of being in the spotlight is ever present—and quite a challenge. So let's shift our focus to principles and skills to manage these situations, and countless others like them, *in public*. Here are some insights into handling the pressure of living in the bright glare of the leadership spotlight.

Accept the Obvious

The first step to becoming more comfortable with the public nature of leadership is to accept the inevitability of your situation. In plain terms, get over it. You may think it's inappropriate for so many people to know about or comment on every aspect of your life. But that won't change the situation. If you are a leader, you have chosen to step into the spotlight. Get used to the glare. Stop whining about how bright it is and how unfair it seems. Doing so is futile and reveals your immaturity and inexperience as a leader.

My first experience on a stage lighted for television was unnerving. The lights were brighter than anything I had previously experienced as a speaker. It was disconcerting being almost blinded by the light. The glare was so intense all I could see were shadows on the first few rows. For a speaker who enjoys audience interaction, not being able to see the crowd was unsettling. My choices were twofold: have the lighting adjusted (not going to happen) or adjust to the situation (quickly adapt to my new reality).

While you may not have expected this much scrutiny, or expected your family to be subjected to it as well, leadership is a public responsibility. Being a leader means people are interested in your life—not only your professional life but your personal life as well. While you should create boundaries to separate your private life from your public life, your followers won't see those boundaries as clearly as you would like. Railing against this is counterproductive. Accept the reality your life will be lived on stage, in public, with many interested spectators. Learning essential skills to thrive in this environment is much better than wasting energy complaining about it or wishing it would change. Besides, as a Christian leader, you lead with your life as much as with words, ideas, and vision. This not only comes with the territory, it *is* the territory.

Don't Play to the Crowd

The temptation, since leaders have an inescapable audience, is to play to the crowd—performing to please people, thus minimizing your followers' negative impressions and comments. Succumbing to that temptation, however, has devastating, long-range consequences because it ignores "the doctrine of the crowd." The doctrine of the crowd can be summarized this way: Crowds are fickle, can't be trusted, and often believe the last voice they hear. Consider what happened to Paul and Barnabas on their mission trip to Lystra.

The missionary team had a rough time in Iconium (Acts 14:1–7) prior to arriving in Lystra. Their work in the Iconian synagogue was initially fruitful, but ultimately resulted in both Jews and Gentiles opposing them. When Paul and Barnabas learned of a plot to stone them, they fled to Lystra. Their ministry there opened with a remarkable healing of a man lame from birth. On Paul's command, he jumped up and started to walk around. It was a dramatic example of the power of God confirming Paul's preaching (vv. 8–10).

The story continues, "When the crowds saw what Paul had done, they raised their voices, saying in the Lycaonian language, 'The gods have come down to us in the form of men!' And they started to call Barnabas, Zeus, and Paul, Hermes, because he was the main speaker. Then the priest of Zeus, whose temple was just outside the town, brought oxen and garlands to the gates. He, with the crowds, intended to offer sacrifice" (vv. 11–13).

Now that's more like it! Paul and Barnabas were called gods and received accolades for their ability to work miracles and preach truth. Who wouldn't prefer that kind of reception rather than being stoned? Be honest. Wouldn't you like, just once, for your followers to erupt in riotous, tumultuous applause celebrating your spiritual power and wisdom? While "oxen and garlands" would be a bit much, a generous bonus or a special gift would be a welcome expression of support. Leaders are human and something deep within us longs for the approval of others. We want the crowd to like us. We want our followers to appreciate us.

Paul and Barnabas had both the spiritual sense and personal discipline to resist being worshipped (vv. 14–18). They "tore their robes" both to signify their grief and reveal their human bodies as they shouted, "We are men also." With significant effort, "they barely stopped the crowds from sacrificing to them" (v. 18).

Would you have had the discernment and discipline to short-circuit that celebration? Keep in mind, even though it was early in their missionary careers, Paul and Barnabas had already been subjected to intense opposition (Acts 13:44–45, 50; 14:4–6). Finally, they had arrived in a city that welcomed them and their message. More than welcoming them, the Lystrans added Paul and Barnabas to the pantheon of gods they worshipped. And even more, they were willing to worship them as preeminent members of the pantheon—Zeus and Hermes. If you had recently been rebuked and assaulted, the prospect of being worshipped (even just a little) would be a powerful temptation. But what happened next in the story is a sobering reminder not to believe what the crowds say about you.

Within a few days, "some Jews came from Antioch and Iconium, and when they had won over the crowds and stoned Paul, they dragged him out of the city, thinking he was dead" (Acts 14:19). The same crowds that had worshipped Paul and Barnabas were now whipped into a destructive frenzy. They stoned Paul, dragged him out of the city, and left him for dead. This exemplifies the doctrine of the crowd—fickle people easily influenced to impulsive action. While Paul had been praised for his preaching accompanied by miracles, some latter-day influencers "won over the crowds" and convinced them to attack the men they had formerly revered. Like many crowds, the last voice they heard carried the day and instigated their negative behavior.

While you lead in public, be careful not to trust the opinion of the crowd—good or bad, positive or negative—nor allow it to control your behavior. Since followers will voice opinions about everything from your wardrobe to your parenting style to your car choice to your speaking ability, it's easy to be influenced by what they say. It's easy to be overly discouraged by the critics or made overly confident by your supporters. Either way, you are giving in to crowd mentality. Resist the temptation to go along with the crowd and its opinion of you. Resist the temptation to develop your security, your inner sense of well-being and acceptance, from the opinion of others. Look to a far better source of security than the fickle whim of your followers.

Develop Security in Jesus Christ

The essential spiritual quality enabling you to be yourself in the spotlight and resist being controlled by the expectations of others is security. While I have written in more detail about this important subject in my book *The Character of Leadership*, let's focus specifically here on the importance of developing security for leading in the public eye.

The desires for security and significance are not sub-Christian. God has made every person with the same basic desires and drives. There is nothing wrong with wanting to feel secure. The problem is, we often satisfy this deep longing in destructive ways. The solution isn't eradicating your need to feel secure. The solution is finding security from the right source.

Finding security is essential for leaders because it's the source of peace and rest, of being comfortable in your own skin. Having peace with God and from God gives us peace with ourselves and within ourselves. The greater our public responsibility, the larger the crowd that observes us, the more essential is this important spiritual quality. God's peace is often the difference between calm and calamity when facing a leadership challenge.

A basic doctrine of the Christian faith is the security of the believer. My limited initial understanding of this doctrine ("once saved, always saved") made me think it was more about tomorrow than it is about today. But my longing for security as a young leader drove me to reconsider this doctrine. After significant study, this breakthrough came: *The security of the believer is as much about today as it is about eternity.* The security of the believer means every person who trusts Jesus for salvation will always be secure in him and with him. But it also means we are as secure now as we will ever be. Your security in Jesus isn't something you get when you die. You received it when you were saved. You are as secure in Jesus right now as you will ever be.

The security of the believer isn't a cold, sterile doctrine to be debated. It's a present spiritual reality to be enjoyed. Your security in Jesus Christ, now and forever, is the bedrock for maintaining your spiritual, emotional, and psychological equilibrium for public leadership. The beginning point of overcoming insecurity is renewing your mind with biblical truth about your security in Jesus. Your security as a believer, particularly as it relates to leadership, can be experienced by living out this key doctrine.

God and Jesus make you secure.

In John 10:28–29, believers are described as being held tightly in Jesus's hands. Jesus and all believers are portrayed as being held tightly in God's hands. Jesus promises, "no one is able to snatch them out of the Father's hand" and that he and the Father "are one" (v. 30). This imagery means God guarantees your secure relationship with him through Jesus Christ. This simple conviction is the foundation of your security as a believer: God the Father and God the Son hold you securely in relationship with them.

That's comforting! Your security comes from your relationship with God. You aren't responsible for your security, for somehow finding emotional health that produces security, or creating a sense of personal security. You are secure because God has secured you to himself. He has given you identity and infused you with value as his child.

Security emerges, then, from a relationship. We seem to know that intuitively. Seeking security in wrong relationships is the problem. Doing this causes leaders to abuse relationships in a desperate, futile search for security. We may compulsively serve people to gain their approval and blessing (another symptom of succumbing to the doctrine of the crowd). Or we might develop an immoral relationship seeking inner satisfaction and relational fulfillment. In one tragic case, a leader succumbed to the first temptation, which resulted in his wife giving in to the second.

This leader was a compulsive servant. He was always at the beck and call of his church members. He believed, "When the phone rings, I've got to go." No amount of pleading by his wife or counsel from mentors changed his behavior. He was addicted to the sense of well-being he received from his perceived indispensability. He was addicted to crowd approval—to the "attaboys" he received for being Superpastor to give him a sense of security and significance. And because he worked so hard, his crowd grew to an unmanageable size. He spent almost every waking hour doing something for someone.

After several years of this, his wife had an affair. She wasn't a promiscuous person. She was just desperate for security, which she longed for through her husband. Her longing for security through a relationship (unmet through her husband, also unmet through her lover) was misplaced. She made the same mistake, exhibited in different behavior, as her husband. Both pursued security, a sense of well-being and acceptance, through wrong relationships. In the end, a marriage and a ministry were lost because of attempts to meet deep security needs through wrong relationships—he with the crowds, she with another man.

Right principle, wrong applications! You *should* seek security in a relationship but in the right relationship—with God through Jesus. Seeking it in any other relationship— your spouse, child, mother, father, or followers—will leave you empty and longing. Like a sugar high, it may satisfy for a while but will ultimately leave you deflated.

The only source of genuine security is your relationship with God through Jesus. He validates you, blesses you, accepts you, and gives you worth. In him, you *are* secure so you can feel secure and live securely. Many Christian leaders accept the first part of the equation, theological knowledge of security in Jesus, but fewer enjoy the benefits of choosing to live securely in him.

True security resists all threats.

Jesus makes two other promises in John 10:28–29 related to our security. He promises we are so secure "no one" can harm us and we have "eternal life." These promises have two applications related to your security as a leader.

First, no one can take away your security in God through Jesus. You will be tested repeatedly and often at this point by critics, naysayers, and other opponents. Paul and Barnabas probably felt very secure in their relationship with God when his power worked through them to heal the lame man in Lystra. But I wonder if they questioned God's presence when Paul was being stoned, with no miraculous intervention to stop the assault? Circumstances, including unjustified attacks, don't alter our position in God through Christ. We are secure in him.

Second, your security is forever. Remember, it isn't for the afterlife only but for your future in this life as well. Specifically, no matter what the future holds, you are and always will be secure. You can live through public criticism, loss of status, bad decisions, and other personal attacks because you are secure. You can also survive personal loss, family illness, financial setbacks, or whatever else the future has in store for you. Your security in your relationship with God through Jesus can stand up to anything that comes at you.

This is the great, often untapped reality of the security of the believer. You are as secure in Jesus *right now* as you will ever be. You are as secure now as you will someday be in heaven. You *are* secure . . . so live it and enjoy it.

Secure leaders are free to obey God.

When Jesus taught about security, he said that his followers listen to his voice and follow him (John 10:27). Jesus recognized an important reality: People are often controlled by false sources of security. Security is such a strong need, a compelling drive, a powerful thirst, that whoever or whatever satisfies the need will be obeyed. Leaders who draw security from God through Jesus are free to obey God. Leaders who long for security through affirmation from their followers will do whatever necessary to obtain it.

You *will* satisfy your thirst for security. Your inner drive for security isn't the problem. How you satisfy it may be. If your followers' approval makes you feel secure, you will please people at all costs. If accomplishments make you feel secure, you will be driven to get things done. If physical pleasure, however fleeting, gives you a sense of security, you will pursue those passions. You will obey the compelling urge that feeds your need for security. But, if your relationship with God through Jesus is your source of security, you will obey God.

Secure leaders are confident without being arrogant. They are relaxed without being lackadaisical. Secure leaders rest in the reality their relationship with God is their defining source of value, worth, and well-being. They have nothing left to prove, nothing left to conquer, and aren't beholden to anyone. Secure leaders are free to obey God—and there's no greater freedom.

Changing a core belief, like your source of security, happens at both a point in time and as a process over time. It starts by accepting the only legitimate source of security is a relationship with God through Jesus Christ. That's a "point in time" decision you make based on truth—revealed, absolute, nonnegotiable biblical truth.

Hammering down that stake, affirming your conviction about your security, is the first step. The second step is more challenging. You must practice the spiritual discipline of confronting wrong thinking, destructive behavior, and bad habits built on your foundation of false security. You must realize, "Although we are walking in the flesh, we do not wage war in a fleshly way, since the weapons of our warfare are not fleshly, but are powerful through God for the demolition of strongholds. We demolish arguments and every high-minded thing that is raised up against the knowledge of God, taking every thought captive to the obedience of Christ" (2 Cor. 10:3–5).

Implementing these instructions requires meditation, prayer, reflection, accountability, and difficult choices. Foundational to these disciplines is renewing your mind through Scripture memory. Choose key passages about your security in Jesus Christ and commit them to memory. Allow them to reprogram your thinking—to renew your mind—and give you a new outlook on yourself and what gives you true worth. When you do this, real change will come through the new choices you make in your leadership role.

Stick to Your Convictions in Key Areas

Leadership requires convictions. Most leaders demonstrate convictions in church or organizational leadership. But in the spotlight, keeping your convictions in personal areas is also essential to avoid being overwhelmed by the opinions of others. You can't allow your followers to set the agenda for important decisions you make about your family, finances, or personal habits. Doing so initiates a downward spiral of unmet expectations that will leave you frustrated and your family demoralized if they feel you pander to the people instead of protecting their best interests.

Establishing core convictions and sticking to those convictions—no matter what anyone outside your family thinks—is particularly important for leaders in two areas. These key areas are rearing children and managing money. Because these are so vital, let's go into more detail about each area and why it's so important to be convictional, not expedient, in decisions about them. As you read, remember, these are illustrations of the principle of sticking by your core convictions—not a complete guide to parenting or personal finance.

Parenting In Public

Christian leaders are expected, by biblical mandate (1 Tim. 3:4), to be examples of healthy parenting. We aren't expected to be perfect parents nor have perfect children. But we are expected to relate to our children in healthy ways and create a healthy environment (spiritual, emotional, psychological, and physical) for their upbringing.

Ann and I had a core conviction about parenting. We believed our job was to produce emotionally healthy, spiritually growing adults. Once we settled on that mission statement, specific decisions became easier. We were focused on producing adults, which meant we didn't evaluate our children (even as teenagers) based on their behavior in the moment or how anyone else felt about it. We tried our best to make decisions toward our ultimate outcome—emotionally healthy, spiritually growing adults. With that conviction in mind, and the long-term goal in view, we made many difficult parenting decisions. Those decisions were sometimes questioned by people who didn't have all the facts or understand our ultimate objective. Still, we tried our best to resist outside pressure and keep the focus on shaping our children toward adulthood.

As leaders, we knew our parenting practices were being observed by our followers. We knew our actions, like it or not, were being evaluated and often emulated by our followers—especially other young parents. We also knew the mistakes we made and the choices our children made would be criticized. Knowing all this, the temptation was to allow these concerns to determine our parenting practices. We made a conscious effort to resist this subtle pressure and make our decisions based on our core conviction as parents. Again, our mission was emotionally healthy, spiritually growing adults.

We made a sincere effort to make parenting decisions toward accomplishing that purpose—not pleasing our followers or meeting the expectations of others.

Our children are not perfect (and we were far from perfect parents), but our children are now young adults who love Jesus, serve their churches, and value ministry leadership. Like many other church leaders, we had to decide about issues like Sunday sports participation and whether to require our children to attend every youth group activity. We had to handle the awkward situations when our oldest son slugged a girl in Sunday school (they were both six years old) and later when both our sons wanted desperately to quit a children's choir (led by my wife's best friend). We had to decide when dating could start, what public high school events were appropriate, and countless discussions about permissible attire for church events. When the children were small, we sometimes had to deal with defiance and rebellion in public settings. More than one grandmotherly person suggested we were too strict when we reacted firmly to being told "No" by one of our children.

Over the years we made thousands of decisions as parents—some good, some bad. But overall, we did a decent job of keeping the long-term goal in view. We had a core conviction that our job was to produce adults—not perfect children or model teenagers. For that reason we made some decisions that probably puzzled our followers. We endured some criticism from well-meaning folk who wanted the best for our children but didn't share our perspective. We occasionally had to protect our children and help them deal with expectations others projected on them. While we made many mistakes, we did our best to parent by conviction—not expediency in the moment. We tried to parent to accomplish our mission—not to please our followers or be patted on the back for our children's behavior in the moment. We endured some sleepless nights, wondering about some of our decisions, but we never wavered on our core conviction.

This is, in my view, the fundamental decision you must make to parent successfully while living in the public eye. You must establish a core conviction, mission, purpose, or goal (you choose the word that fits your understanding of the concept) for your role as a parent. Then, as best you can, make every decision based on that conviction— not what will please others in the short run. Doing this requires courage, discipline, and occasionally a firm word to reject a follower's persistent suggestions. In the end, your children will be healthier for knowing you parented them by conviction about what was best for their long-term development instead of short-term peace or praise from the cheap seats.

Managing Your Money

Another issue that creates tension for leaders is managing personal finances and their followers' opinions about those choices. Leaders are susceptible to pressure from followers about where they live, where and how they travel, what they wear and drive, and a host of other issues related to lifestyle choices. Christian leaders are also expected to be models of generosity, giving both to the organization they lead and other causes as needed.

Leaders seem to gravitate to two extremes in this area. Some leaders are overly sensitive, cautious about and resistant to expenditures that might be criticized by others. Other leaders make lifestyle choices without regard to their potential negative impact. Somewhere between these two extremes is a healthy balance. Finding that balance, however, will be impossible if you define *balance* as the absence of negative comments by your followers. It just won't happen.

The solution, just like parenting, is establishing core financial convictions and living by them. Going into great detail about financial planning is beyond the scope of this chapter. My focus is helping you manage life in the leadership spotlight—in this case making personal financial decisions that will be scrutinized by others. God has called all believers, including leaders, to be stewards of their financial resources. As a leader, just like every believer, you are responsible to develop a personal stewardship plan that includes giving, saving, and spending. Again, this chapter isn't about how to develop that plan. It's about having the courage to develop a plan and stick to it no matter what people outside your family may think of your choices.

Those choices can be confusing. A few years ago, while having my wife's car serviced, I was browsing a new car showroom. On display was a beautiful sports car—a new model with a price around $35,000. It was gorgeous! As I looked at it, I imagined many of my followers would think I had lost my mind if I made such a purchase. Then I wandered outside to look at new fully loaded, full-size SUVs. The price on one of them was about $45,000. We were living in Oregon at the time, an outdoorsman's paradise where every family seemed to have at least one SUV. As I looked at it, although it cost $10,000 more than the sports car, I imagined many of my followers would think "sweet ride" if I made that purchase.

My car lot musings illustrate this fact—the perceptions people have about your finances and what they mean aren't always based in reality. For that reason, getting too caught up in what people think or say about your financial choices is counterproductive.

On the other hand, there are times when the perceptions of others are significant. One ministry organization provided cars for its senior leaders who drove extensively in their work. A Volvo dealer joined the ministry board and offered to sell the organization new Volvos for the same price the organization was paying for much smaller, less dependable cars. The staff was elated to have this remarkable gift and soon were driving new Volvos. But not for long! Complaints about the cars rolled in from constituents who wondered why a ministry organization supported by their gifts was being so extravagant. At first, the leaders tried to explain the gift. Soon, however, they realized perception, in this case, was undermining their credibility. The Volvos had to go in order to preserve the integrity of the organization in the eyes of their constituents.

So, with such confusing expectations from your followers, how do you manage personal financial decisions? First, make a personal financial plan that takes seriously your stewardship responsibility. Second, stick by your convictions as you implement the plan. Third, ask God for wisdom to help you deal with well-meaning people who put unnecessary pressure on you and your family in this area. Finally, ask God for humility to know when to demonstrate deference so your decisions aren't a stumbling block to others. While these steps won't alleviate all problems in this area, they will give you confidence that you have made a good-faith effort at personal financial responsibility as a leader.

Conclusion

As long as you are a leader, your life will be lived in the spotlight. Your followers and the broader community will observe your professional decisions and personal lifestyle choices. While you can't escape the glare of public scrutiny, you can develop the security you need to withstand the pressure. You can learn to rest in your relationship with God through Jesus. You can learn to live by convictions in key areas, not easily influenced by the crowds nor controlled by their expectations. You can develop and maintain the skills needed to manage these demands, protect your family from any collateral damage of your leadership lifestyle, and handle the challenge of life in the spotlight.

But when you have done your best and persistent critics won't relent, read the next two chapters!

7

Understanding Criticism

Leaders have critics—as surely as dogs have fleas and usually about as helpful! Since having critics is inevitable, learning to handle criticism is an essential skill for leaders to develop. And, make no mistake, it's a skill to develop—not an inherent ability. Our natural tendency, our inborn bent, is to defend ourselves, return the fire, and as a result lose focus on our mission. Resisting these natural impulses requires spiritual discipline and commitment to a better approach. Developing these skills comes from understanding how biblical leaders handled their critics and learning practical ways to implement those principles.

With technology making mass communication easier, critics now have the option of broadcasting their negativity worldwide. In the past, a critic would stop by your office to complain or perhaps write a mean-spirited letter. Now, critics have text messaging, e-mail, blogs, Web sites, and other

electronic means of mass communication available as immediate distribution networks. They also have cheap printers
to mass-produce flyers, newsletters, and other forms of hate
mail. Despite this proliferation of methods, personal insults
are still the most painful. Learning to handle criticism, particularly personal attack, is an essential leadership skill you
must develop.

One biblical leader who endured a personal attack from
a persistent critic was David. His nemesis was a man named
Shimei. Their story begins in 2 Samuel 16 and is foundational for developing the strategies outlined in this chapter
and the next. Shimei's attack is described this way:

> When King David got to Bahurim, a man belong-
> ing to the family of the house of Saul was just
> coming out. His name was Shimei son of Gera,
> and he was yelling curses as he approached. He
> threw stones at David and at all the royal ser-
> vants, the people and the warriors on David's
> right and left. Shimei said as he cursed: "Get
> out, get out, you worthless murderer! The
> LORD has paid you back for all the blood of
> the house of Saul in whose place you rule, and
> the LORD has handed the kingdom over to your
> son Absalom. Look, you are in trouble because
> you're a murderer!" . . . David and his men pro-
> ceeded along the road as Shimei was going along
> the ridge of the hill opposite him. As Shimei
> went, he cursed David and threw stones and dirt
> at him. (vv. 5–8, 13)

Can you imagine this scene? David, while leading his most
loyal followers and family in a hasty retreat, was accosted by

Shimei. He was cursed (cussed out), falsely accused (more about that later), and physically assaulted (stones and dirt hurled down on him). He was attacked publicly, without provocation, in front of both his family and staff (military officers). David's bedraggled party stumbled along—heads down, donkeys (2 Sam. 16:2) dragging with fatigue—while Shimei angrily (and it seems, gleefully) shouted curses and hurled stones at them. What a depressing and pathetic picture of a critical attack on a once potent monarch.

Before looking at how David handled his critic and what we can learn from his example (in the next chapter), let's consider the characteristics of criticism revealed by this story. As you will see, while the names and places have changed, the vitriolic methods of modern critics closely resemble those of their ancient ancestors. In this case, the more things change—the more they stay the same.

Criticism Often Comes When We Least Need It

When Shimei cursed him, David was already at a low point in both his family life and career. David had allowed a significant family conflict to go unresolved. It had festered, tearing his family apart and threatening his legacy. Three years before this infamous retreat, David's daughter, Tamar, had been raped by her half brother, David's son Amnon (2 Sam. 13:1–21). In retaliation, another of David's sons, Absalom, had killed Amnon (2 Sam. 13:22–38). Absalom then fled into exile for three years and built a power base to overthrow David and assume his throne. Absalom had completed the coup, resulting in David's retreat with his fragmented family and a small army of loyal followers.

David had also recently heard Mephibosheth had deserted him and remained in Jerusalem to support Absalom (2 Sam. 16:3). Mephibosheth was Jonathan's crippled son, whom David had essentially adopted (because of his profound friendship with Jonathan and loyalty to Saul's household). Mephibosheth lived in the palace and was treated like a favored son, eating at the king's table and enjoying David's protection (2 Sam. 9). While it would later be proved Mephibosheth had remained loyal to David, at the time of Shimei's attack David didn't know that to be true (2 Sam. 19:24–29).

David not only had family problems, he had significant problems at work—in his case, as a dethroned king. He had lost his kingdom—a major problem! His army was in disarray, his leadership was compromised, his treasury had been looted, and his palace confiscated. David's career was in shambles. He was a king without a throne and a commander in chief without an army. Combine this with his family problems, and the last thing David needed was an attack from a mean-spirited, rock-throwing critic.

Criticism often comes when we least need it. When we moved to Oregon to start a new church, we were emotionally and spiritually vulnerable. We had given up life among friends and financial stability and had moved across the country, risking our family's well-being and our careers. One Sunday a vacationing couple from a large, well-established church in the Bible Belt visited our morning worship service. After the service, held in a rented school gym, the man said to me, "You are a good speaker. Someday, if you keep it up, maybe someone will give you a real church." *A real church.* Those words cut deeply. I wanted to scream out, "This is a real church." Instead, I muttered, "Maybe someday," and merely walked away. Those words still sting. Insensitive criticism because we weren't *a real church* was the last thing I needed to hear as we struggled every week to carve a new church out of the granitelike secularism of the Pacific Northwest.

It's uncanny how often a critic will attack when you are emotionally depleted by other struggles. One critic sent me a series of blistering letters while I was dealing with a serious illness in my extended family and simultaneously helping one of my children through a difficult time. The last thing I needed, while coping with those personal crises, was a critical attack. In football, they call it "piling on" when a person jumps on a tackled player after he is already down. Leaders know the pain of managing personal struggles, while at the same time being piled-on by a critic.

Remember, criticism often comes when you least need it.

Criticism Often Comes When We Least Deserve It

Shimei made two specific accusations against David that were blatant lies. He accused David of shedding the blood of Saul's household and of usurping Saul's throne (2 Sam. 16:8). Neither was true. In fact, David had carefully avoided harming Saul or taking the throne prematurely.

David had at least two opportunities to take Saul's life. The first was during an encounter in a cave (1 Sam. 24:1–7) when David was close enough to cut off a piece of Saul's robe. The second was when David sneaked into Saul's camp (1 Sam. 26:1–11) and stole his spear and water jug. Twice David was close enough to kill Saul but wouldn't lift his hand "against the LORD's anointed" (as he often referred to Saul). Despite Shimei's claims, David had never harmed Saul and had taken great pains to preserve his life. And when Saul was killed, David mourned his death and took the life of Saul's slayer (2 Sam. 1:1–16) rather than celebrate becoming king by that means.

The second accusation against David was also baseless. Samuel had anointed David as the future king, indicating God's choice in the matter (1 Sam. 16:1–13). David didn't immediately become king. It was a slow process, waiting for Saul's reign to end and David's to begin. David waited about twenty years from his anointing to his coronation (2 Sam. 5:1–5). There was no truth to Shimei's criticism that David had inappropriately advanced his rule at Saul's expense. The facts make Shimei's criticism absurd.

Criticism often comes when we least deserve it. When writing my doctoral project report, the seminary required careful preparation of the final paper. It had to be in precise Turabian form. I took that counsel seriously. When it came time for typing the final draft, I employed a supposed Turabian expert and trusted her with the finished product. I submitted it confidently only to receive a letter telling me the entire three-hundred-page document was rejected, along with a stinging rebuke for not taking seriously the instructions about submitting it in proper form. I was embarrassed, humiliated at being criticized for something I had spent more than a year trying to write correctly. I was angry; frustrated I had spent several hundred dollars on a wasted "expert" and received only stinging criticism for my effort.

I had taken every reasonable step to submit the report in the appropriate form. That it was unacceptable was a shocking surprise. My typist had botched the job, but since it was my paper, the criticism rightly landed squarely on my shoulders. Even though I had done all I could to guarantee an acceptable report, it had been summarily rejected. After a major reformatting (and in those days, onerous retyping), it was finally accepted. But the criticism still stung. Sometimes you make a sincere effort to do a good job and you still get criticized.

One significant area stands out as a frequent source of undeserved criticism for leaders—personnel issues. Whether you are managing volunteers in a small church or dozens of employees in a larger organization, making personnel decisions and handling the aftermath of a dismissal can result in undeserved criticism. Both employment law (for paid personnel) and Christian ethics (for employees and volunteers) prohibit leaders from revealing the reasons an employee or volunteer is demoted, terminated, or reassigned. Yet the employee or volunteer doesn't have those same restrictions. In short, the person impacted often has a lot to say about his or her side of the story while you must remain silent. Friends and associates of dismissed employees are often eager to believe their version of events and take up their cause.

Several times, when dismissing employees, I have paid severance when it wasn't deserved or allowed a resignation when termination was in order only to be criticized by outsiders as callous, unfair, unforgiving, judgmental, or meanspirited. The "you are just another example of Christians shooting their wounded" line has been used so often it seems like part of a script written for these scenarios. Hearing these criticisms, particularly when you know the rest of the story, is tough. But revealing all you know and the reasons for your actions isn't an option. Doing so is unethical and self-serving. You can't compromise your integrity by sharing inappropriate information, even when it would clarify matters in your favor.

Remember, criticism often comes when you least deserve it.

Criticism Often Comes from Those Least Qualified to Give It

Who was this fellow Shimei? He is described with three qualifying phrases in the Bible. He was from Saul's clan (a distant cousin), the son of Gera, from a place called Bahurim. His familial connection to Saul is interesting but of no consequence. He was simply related to someone famous, like a person today claiming to be a distant cousin of an athlete or entertainer. Shimei's father, Gera, is never mentioned in the Bible except in this story and has no apparent historical significance. Bahurim, likewise, isn't prominent in biblical history. So Shimei was a nobody from nowhere with no significant contribution worthy of mention in the Bible. If it weren't for being an infamous critic, he wouldn't have been included in the biblical narrative. Yet, despite his obscure status and historical insignificance, he attacked David—one of the greatest men in biblical history—and compounded David's misfortune with his withering criticism.

It's amazing how some people think they know everything about you—how you should lead, preach, raise your children, dress, manage your money; where you should live; what you should drive; whom you should hire and how you should supervise them. There are so many experts who know so much about perfecting our supposed shortcomings. As my wife jokes, "God loves you, but everyone else has a wonderful plan for your life!"

When we first started in pastoral ministry, my wife had a critic who frequently pointed out her supposed deficiencies and inadequacies. At first, these seemed like well-intended suggestions. But over time they progressed to more pointed critiques and personal attacks. Finally Ann started declining the "let's get together and talk" invitations because she knew they were thinly veiled attempts to further correct her shortcomings. As Ann's availability diminished, her critic resorted to writing letters pointing out her needed improvements. It became wearisome. We dreaded seeing this woman's handwriting on an envelope. We knew what was inside—more criticism usually couched in spiritual words and preachy platitudes about "wanting what's best for you as a pastor's wife."

Ann's critic had never been a pastor's wife. She had no personal experience with the pressures, expectations, and demands of trying to balance church activities, family priorities, and the various expectations of church members. Yet she felt qualified to offer counsel about how to do these things better. She was unqualified but nonetheless insistent and persistent in her attempts to correct my wife. There is a "rest of the story" about this critic—stay tuned for it in the next chapter.

Pastoral leaders, more than leaders in other professions, seem particularly susceptible to armchair quarterbacks. The same people who would never lecture their doctor or correct their attorney are quite free with suggestions for their pastor. Because they rightly believe every Christian is a minister, they assume they know how *to lead* a ministry.

Because church members and pastors live in close community, it's easy for parishioners to assume they know as much about their fellow church members as the pastor does. And, because pastors usually turn the other cheek, some critics feel little restraint in letting their pastor know exactly how he could do his job better by heeding their advice.

Remember, criticism often comes from those least qualified to give it.

Criticism Often Comes as a Personal Attack

Shimei's assault on David was personal. It was directed at him when he was vulnerable and attempted to humiliate him. Not only did Shimei throw rocks and dirt, he cursed David. Getting cussed out is very personal. The childhood ditty "sticks and stones may break my bones, but words will never hurt me" is false. Harsh words hurt. Having your character attacked, your family demeaned, your work devalued, and your decisions belittled is painful. Many adults struggle with harmful words spoken by their mother or father—words seared into their soul that have largely determined their self-worth and destiny. Leaders, particularly younger leaders, can be permanently scarred by harsh words spoken by critics.

My first ministry position was as a minister to children. As part of our activities program, our boys entered a track meet organized by the churches in our area. Several hundred boys participated in front of a large crowd at a local stadium. The day before the event, the starting time was unexpectedly moved up one hour. I called every boy I could reach (long before answering machines) and told them of the change. One boy was on a family camping trip and couldn't be contacted. He arrived late, after several of his events had already been contested. When his mother realized what had happened, she came around the end of the grandstand and everyone knew she had arrived because she shrieked my name, "Jeff Iorg!" Several hundred people sat down to watch the show.

She dressed me down, verbally assaulting me for causing her son to miss his events and upbraiding me for my irresponsibility and failure as a leader of young men. I was speechless (not common for me!) and just stood there and absorbed her barrage. When she finished, she stomped off before I could offer any explanation. It was a painful, humiliating experience.

A few months later a similar event happened. Our weekday child-care program changed its policies to no longer accept part-time children. We only had two part-time children in our program of more than one hundred daily attendees. When we announced the change, we allowed several months for both families to find alternate care. But when one of the mothers learned of the change, she stormed into my office, lectured me on my insensitivity to her needs, leaned over my desk (I can still see her fiery eyes!), and hissed through clenched teeth, "And you call yourself a minister." With that, she stomped out, slamming the door behind her.

Those incidents happened almost thirty years ago, yet the memories are still vivid. The pain has healed, but the scars remain. Critics attack personally, tearing us down, humiliating us, demeaning our efforts, and attacking our identity as Christians, leaders, or ministers. Words hurt. Harsh words penetrate and scar. Feelings of inadequacy and condemnation settle into our souls and drain spiritual and emotional energy. Critics make it personal, and we carry their words with us for a long time.

On top of this, leaders personify the church or the organization they lead. This means you take the heat for the shortcomings of your church or ministry organization and the performance of your employees or volunteer staff. Oftentimes, critics voice their displeasure and hold me responsible when I had no idea a problem even existed. That salient fact, however, doesn't seem to deter many critics. The leader personifies the organization and is responsible for the actions of everyone associated with it. The larger your leadership responsibility the more likely you will be criticized, personally, for the actions of others.

Remember, criticism often comes as a personal attack.

When Critics Become Criminals

Shimei's actions, if they happened today, would be criminal acts. Lying about a person is slander. Publishing lies is libel. Physically attacking another person is assault. Critics sometimes go beyond verbal and written attacks and threaten or inflict physical harm. For example, when one critic was recognized to speak in a congregational meeting, a pastor expected the worst—and got even more than he dreaded. The critic came to the podium, but instead of turning to speak to the church, he slugged the pastor in the face. In another case, an employee in a Christian organization was very critical of his coworkers. One day he complained about being treated unfairly and announced he was going home to get his shotgun and come back to solve the problem once for all. Police intervention perhaps prevented a massacre. One megachurch pastor and his wife have received repeated death threats. Church-employed security personnel shadow them every Sunday.

Another pastor (of a medium-sized church in a small city) and his family have been victimized by a stalker for seven years . . . and counting. The woman visited his church and was ultimately led to faith in Jesus Christ by the pastor. Soon thereafter, she informed the pastor she was in love with him, they were destined for each other, and she would do anything to be with him. At first, it seemed like misplaced affection, a harmless infatuation. The pastor, his wife, and other church leaders met with the woman to confront her and counsel her about her delusions.

But within a few weeks, the obsessive behavior turned ugly. She determined that God told her to have a romantic relationship with the pastor. Over the next few months, she wrote letters, sent e-mail, trailed the pastor in the community, and sought opportunities to be alone with him. She also staked out his family—following his wife while shopping or at work and spying on their children at school or playing in their neighborhood. Eventually the pastor's family and church leaders reached the end of their ability to handle the situation and asked law enforcement to intervene. The woman was arrested and charged with stalking.

When authorities entered her home, they were shocked. One wall in her house was covered with photos of the pastor and his family members. The photos were candid photos, taken without their knowledge while the family was at work, school, shopping, or church. The police found evidence the woman had been inside the pastor's home. There was also a shooting silhouette with some bullet holes in it (labeled with the pastor's wife's name).

When the stalker's computer was analyzed, it contained hundreds of e-mails and letters she had written but never sent. They chronicled further plans to ensnare the pastor and displace his wife. It was also discovered she had hacked the church's computer system and was privy to the pastor's calendar, personal information, and private e-mail accounts. There was physical evidence she had broken into the church's offices.

The stalker was convicted and sent to jail where she received a mental health evaluation and treatment. She was released after a few months and soon resumed her former pattern. By then, the church had instituted a comprehensive security plan to protect the pastor, his family, and the congregation from possible violence. And, as anticipated, the stalking resumed and was even more threatening. The warnings about harming the pastor's wife and children turned into promises of impending action. The pastor's family was sent away while the police continued to monitor the stalker's behavior and determine a course of action. When they returned, the threats intensified, and the stalker was once again arrested, convicted, and sent to jail.

While she was imprisoned, the authorities reluctantly admitted they were unable to stop the cycle of stalking, short-term incarceration, and intensified threats. They asked the pastor's family to consider entering a witness protection program, to change their identities, and relocate to another community. While they appreciated the efforts of the law enforcement community to protect them, they declined the offer because they doubted their ability (particularly their children's ability) to disappear without a trace. They knew if there was any possibility the stalker could find them—she would.

The stalker is very intelligent but mentally ill—having been diagnosed and treated while in jail. She responds to treatment in order to secure release when her sentence is served. Like many mentally ill people, however, she discontinues her treatment plan when not under supervision and resumes former patterns of behavior. In her case, she is fixated on having a romantic relationship with the pastor and seems capable of almost any action to facilitate her obsession.

This family now lives in a security bubble. The police regularly patrol both the church facility and the pastor's neighborhood. The church has a security plan and has installed a video/electronic surveillance system. Staff at the schools the children attend are briefed annually on the threat and taught to recognize the stalker in various disguises. Neighbors have been briefed and help create a safe environment for the children—a place to ride bikes, skate, and hang out with friends. Finally the pastor and his wife carry concealed weapons and have been trained in self-defense.

If you have a critic engaging in potentially criminal behavior, this beleaguered pastor would give the following advice. First, document everything. Keep a time line, communication log, and diary of both the critic's actions and your responses (his documentation is the basis for this section). Second, involve law enforcement and do what these officials tell you to do. They exist for your protection (Rom. 13), and involving them to stop criminal behavior doesn't violate the biblical prohibition on civil lawsuits among believers. Third, recognize that you may be dealing with a mentally ill person who needs medical treatment. While this doesn't mean you don't take decisive action, it does mean you can't expect a reasoned conclusion. It may be messy for a long time. Fourth, protect your family. Inform school officials and neighbors about the situation and don't understate its seriousness. Don't succumb to the temptation to minimize this information to protect the person threatening you. Tell everyone everything, and ask for everyone's help. Finally, guide your church or organization to develop a strategic response plan and adequate security measures for a worst-case scenario. While the threat may be directed at you, the collateral damage of an armed attacker will harm many. Church members or organizational employees also need protection. Time and money spent on prevention may save lives and millions of settlement dollars in case of a violent attack.

When the Tables Are Turned

Thankfully most leaders don't have this kind of intense situation to manage on a daily basis. Aren't you glad your worst problem is an aggressive blogger or a bitter former employee? Knowing the pastor in the situation described above has helped change my perspective on my critics. Mine aren't this aggressive and can be handled much more easily. My critics have taught me another important lesson. They mirror my behavior. Sometimes I'm a critic. Just as criticism from others hurts me, my criticism of others hurts them. My critics have helped me be less critical. No genuine Christian leader enjoys inflicting painful criticism.

Unfortunately my past attacks on others have all the characteristics of criticism described above—minus the stalker! There was the time I drop-kicked a watercooler in a baseball dugout and yelled at my assistant coach in front of the team.

It was an undeserved and badly timed personal attack on a young man who looked up to me. There was the time (OK, the *times*) I have lectured my wife about preschool ministry operations (her passion and expertise). Those criticisms were unnecessary, undeserved, and clearly from someone unqualified to give them. There was the time I wrote the president of my university (while I was still a student) and harangued him about his facilitation of the spiritual hypocrisy on campus. It was misguided (at best), arrogant (at worst), and from someone completely unqualified to critique a university leader. How ironic I now receive those same kinds of letters! When one comes, my response is tempered by memories of my impetuosity and youthful zeal, which prompted my letter. Sometimes, even when we know how much it hurts we are still critical of others. But as God has allowed me to be criticized, in ways too painful or personal to put in these pages, my tendency to criticize others has diminished. And that is a good thing!

Conclusion

As we return to the story of David and Shimei (in the next chapter), David's response to his attacker becomes instructive for us. There are several helpful principles revealed by David's actions. The story takes some surprising turns as it plays out over several years to a dramatic conclusion. So let's shift our focus in the next chapter from understanding criticism to effectively handling a critic.

8

Handling Criticism

As a young minister, the pastor who mentored me did a good job protecting me from criticism. My many mistakes certainly caused him problems, but he seldom told me about them. He knew young leaders are like new plants. They need support until they are mature enough to withstand storm winds. He was also circumspect about sharing criticism he received about his leadership. He wanted me to think the best of our followers. He avoided sharing information that might have jaded my perspective. And because of my profound respect for my pastor, it never crossed my mind to criticize him. This was my idyllic experience as a young leader.

And then I became a pastor.

Within months, critics emerged to correct, cajole, and condemn me for my actions, motives, and results. What a shock! Having been sheltered, perhaps even overprotected during my early years in ministry, I had a rude awakening to discover the reality of the criticism a Christian leader endures. I was unprepared for the abrupt change, for people commenting so freely and so negatively about my leadership.

Looking back, I realize my problem with criticism was threefold and largely fueled by unrealistic expectations (remember chapter 2—having realistic expectations about ministry is essential). First, I made a lot of mistakes (like most young leaders), and criticism naturally resulted. I should have expected it, but I didn't. Second, my unrealistic view of how my mentor-pastor had handled criticism left me ill equipped to handle it myself. I assumed, since he didn't talk about his critics, he didn't have any. He is still a friend and has repeatedly assured me that wasn't the case. And third, I expected my followers to share my on-a-pedestal view of pastors and treat me the same way.

Those were naive, unrealistic expectations. A more realistic perspective would have made handling those struggles easier. Admitting Christian leaders are criticized unmasks a hidden reality about ministry leadership. Like most secrets, exposing this one defangs it and makes handling criticism easier. Criticism hurts. It's painful to be insulted, have your motives questioned, or have your ministry skills doubted. But knowing it's coming and learning strategies to manage your critics takes some of the sting out of their criticism. In the previous chapter, we analyzed the nature of criticism by considering Shimei, a critic who attacked David verbally and physically. Now let's return to the story to learn strategies to handle your critics.

Remember the setting of the story. David was having a difficult time. He had lost his kingdom to his son Absalom. His army was in disarray. He had abandoned his palace and was fleeing for his life with his family and a small band of loyal soldiers. As they went along, Shimei paralleled David's traveling party along an adjoining ridgeline. Shimei cursed David and threw rocks and dirt down on him and his companions.

This attack was completely undeserved and inappropriate. The criticism came at a vulnerable time for David. He was criticized for things he didn't do, attitudes he didn't have, actions he hadn't taken, and results he hadn't caused. The attack was both verbal and physical. It was personal and public. Based on David's response, we can safely assume it was painful—emotionally, spiritually, and physically. Yet, in the midst of the attack, David's response is instructive for handling criticism that comes your way.

Respond, Don't React, to Your Critics

David had a soldier with him named Abishai. He was one of David's "mighty men" who closely guarded the king and was often with David in various battles and other conflict situations. While Shimei was cursing and throwing rocks and dirt, Abishai became livid at the insult David was enduring. He had committed his life to defending David, and now a nobody from nowhere was verbally and physically assaulting his king.

His rage erupted when he said to David, "Why should this dead dog curse my lord the king? Let me go over and cut his head off" (2 Sam. 16:9). Now, *that* is the way to handle a critic! Abishai is one of my favorite biblical characters. Every time he is mentioned in the Bible, he was either organizing for battle, killing someone, or asking for permission to kill someone (1 Sam. 26:6–9; 2 Sam. 2:17–24; 3:30;

10:10–14; 16:5–9; 18:2; 19:18–21; 20:6–10; 21:17; 23:18; 1 Chron. 11:20; 18:12; 19:11–15). He was a warrior with one mission—defend the king's honor.

Oh, how I have sometimes wished for an Abishai on my team! I have fantasized about an Abishai taking care of my critics. I don't mean every critic has to *die*—a maiming or mauling would be sufficient. But it would be great to retaliate, to just once make life as painful for my critics as they have made life for me.

The problems with retaliation, however, are manifold. First, retaliation is never a clean process. When you attack a critic, you lower yourself to his level. When you slap a pig, you get muddy. When you attack a critic, you can be bloodied. Second, retaliation violates Jesus's command to love your enemies and pray for people who abuse you (Matt. 5:43–45). Not returning an attack is one way to demonstrate love. And third, retaliation just doesn't work. Efforts to retaliate against a critic leave you emotionally deflated, spiritually discouraged, and usually with a bigger mess than before your efforts to even the score.

A few years ago a person sent me a critical e-mail, accusing me of doctrinal error and criticizing me for associating with a prominent pastor who was (in his opinion) leading people away from biblical Christianity. Both accusations were far off base, almost ludicrous. In a fit of anger and bad judgment, I took up the battle and reacted to the attack. Bad decision! The writer took my e-mail answer, edited it to suit his purposes, and created a blog site to defame me and the pastor he opposed. What started as a simple written response turned into additional ammunition for the attacker to post an "I told you so" entry on his attack Web site.

Reacting to critics usually involves three aspects—trying to explain your actions, trying to justify your motives, and trying to argue the issues to your advantage. None of this works. Why not? Because most critics have their minds made up when they attack you. They are judge, jury, and executioner. They aren't attempting dialogue with you. Their purpose is to take their shots, do their damage, and move on to other prey. So, reacting to critics is never helpful.

Abishai reacted to Shimei. David did not. He made a *response*—a carefully reasoned, spiritually seasoned *response*. His response involved four aspects—focus, reflection, an appropriate reply, and developing a long-term strategy for managing a difficult person. Consider these steps as you develop a strategy for responding to critics.

Stay Focused on Your Mission

When a critic is fully engaged, it's difficult to ignore him. Shimei certainly had Abishai's undivided attention. It's easy to imagine him riding behind David, glaring up at Shimei, fingering his sword, and hoping David would change his mind. His request to behead the pip-squeak reveals his focus on what he perceived to be their most pressing problem.

David, on the other hand, had a more significant enemy and the more significant problem in view. David was focused on Absalom (who had taken his kingdom) and was now attempting to take his life. David reminded Abishai and the traveling party, "Look, my own son, my own flesh and blood, intends to take my life—how much more now this Benjaminite!" (2 Sam. 16:11). In other words, David knew his real problem was Absalom, the lost kingdom, and the genuine threat on his life that existed until Absalom was stopped. The real problem was Absalom—not some curse-shouting, rock-throwing, self-righteous critic.

David's response illustrates two principles for every leader in handling criticism. First, know your mission and stay resolutely focused on it. Second, identify the true obstacles to accomplishing your mission and focus on overcoming them. In David's case, the mission was reclaiming his kingdom. The obstacle was Absalom's armed revolt. Overcoming the coup was the means to accomplishing the mission. David had resolute focus on his mission as well as the true obstacle in the way of accomplishing it. No critic would be able to distract him from his laserlike focus. Absalom had to be stopped. The kingdom had to be reclaimed.

A clearly articulated mission is a powerful asset when you face criticism. The greater the responsibility you bear, the more significant it is to have a clearly defined mission. This is particularly true because the greater your responsibility, usually the greater amount of criticism you will receive. One executive for a professional sports franchise makes personnel decisions for his team. He has a high-profile position, and his decisions are played out in public. He is frequently lampooned—newspapers, blogs, and talk radio—for the team's perceived shortcomings. Criticism is an inevitable part of his job, but maintaining mission clarity (obtaining the best players possible) keeps him from being discouraged by every armchair executive who "knows just what the team should do."

As a seminary president, I have learned one of the unwritten roles of seminaries is to take the blame. Take the blame for what? Everything wrong in the kingdom! For example, when baptisms are down—the seminaries should do a better job of teaching students to witness. When missions go through giving slumps—the seminaries should do a better job of teaching future pastors about leading churches to give. When a doctrinal problem arises—the seminaries should do a better job of grounding people in the Word. When there aren't enough missionaries—the seminaries should do a better job of presenting the call to missions. When a pastor is terminated—the seminaries should do a better job of teaching future pastors to preach, work more effectively with people, manage change, cast vision, or whatever the cause of that particular firing.

Someone has to take the blame for shortcomings of ministry leaders and poor church results. So seminaries are the unofficial blame-takers for problems across the kingdom. Responding to these criticisms would be a full-time job. It would immobilize us through constant stopping and starting, changing and adjusting, accommodating and conciliating. Doing this would paralyze us and rob us of mission focus.

Leading your school, church, or organization requires disciplined focus on your mission. Every critic can't be right; every suggestion can't be heeded. If you attempt to adjust your organization to accommodate every critic, all momentum will be lost. If you continually change your mission, followers and employees will become discouraged and lose interest in the sacrificial service required in ministry organizations. Good leaders absorb criticism, deflect and deflate its influence away from team members, passionately pursue their mission, and lead their organization to do the same.

How can you do this? One key step in maintaining mission focus is controlling the agenda in meetings, personal conversations, and communications. For example, set a written agenda for leadership team meetings. The agenda should almost never include acknowledging critics. Don't let them on your agenda, much less set your agenda. Don't give them the time of day. Focus on your mission, on actions to accomplish your mission, and genuine obstacles to overcome along the way. This can be very difficult when the attacks are widely known. Nevertheless, an agenda focused on the mission helps keep a team on track.

Another aspect of maintaining mission focus is controlling what you talk about in various settings. Part of a leader's discipline is not allowing critics to become gossip fodder for hallway conversations. This can be difficult. Wanting to share juicy gossip, have a big laugh at your critic's expense, or otherwise make light of the situation is tempting. We all like to talk about other people—particularly colorful people who attack us in creative ways. Making this simple choice, avoiding casual conversations about your critics, will help you and your team stay focused on your mission.

This also extends to your family. Don't share every negative experience, attack, or encounter with your spouse or children. Every leader needs someone to whom he can vent frustrations. But doing it at home isn't healthy. Find a friend, colleague, or mentor. Pay a counselor. Hire a consultant. Talk to your board chairman. But don't dump this mess on your family. It isn't fair to them or healthy for shaping their view of ministry leadership.

Finally, monitor other communication venues and limit time given to critics in those as well. Newsletters, church bulletins, blogs, and Web sites are all tempting venues to write about critics. Doing so will only distract your followers and give credence to critics who might otherwise have remained unknown without the publicity you provide.

Remember, followers assume what a leader communicates is important. If your critics are frequent subject matter for your meetings, conversations, and organizational communication—you can expect your followers to divert attention to them rather than focusing on the mission. Keep critics from robbing you of mission focus by controlling communication about their criticism.

Find God's Good in Every Criticism

Until now, we have taken a mostly negative view of critics and criticism. And, to be sure, most of their actions are negative, hurtful, and counterproductive. But God has the power to bring good out of every circumstance and promises "all things work together for the good of those who love God: those who are called according to His purpose" (Rom. 8:28). It may surprise you to learn God can use your critics for good in your life.

Returning to David's response to Shimei, consider his spiritual perspective on the situation. David recognized, even though they were inappropriate and hurtful, Shimei's curses were allowed by God. David said, "He curses me this way because the LORD told him, 'Curse David!' Therefore, who can say, 'Why did you do that?' . . . Leave him alone and let him curse me; the LORD has told him to" (2 Sam. 16:10–11). David believed God had permitted Shimei to attack him and, in light of that, wasn't willing to question whether or not it should have happened.

David also expected good results from the attack. He said, "Perhaps the LORD will see my affliction and restore goodness to me instead of Shimei's curses today" (2 Sam. 16:12). While it's hard to imagine making this kind of faith affirmation while being cursed and pelted, David maintained hope that God was in control of the situation and would bring good out of it.

Remember Joseph? He was sold into slavery by his brothers, falsely accused of rape, imprisoned for years, and finally rose to leadership in Egypt. Ultimately Joseph reunited his entire extended family under his care. When his father finally died, his brothers feared for their lives. They were concerned Joseph would take retribution on them for their crime against him and all the trouble it had brought. But to their surprise, Joseph affirmed, "You planned evil against me; God planned it for good to bring about the present result—the survival of many" (Gen. 50:20). The Joseph principle is this: What people do to harm us, God uses to bless us and others.

God has worked through critics to do several good things in my life. That's hard to write, and it has been harder to experience. God works, even through critics, to shape our character, refine our motives, and otherwise teach us truth we couldn't learn by any other means. Here are some examples, by no means an exhaustive list, to get you thinking about how God might use your critics in a positive way.

God can change you at the point of criticism.

One of my early criticisms from various sources was my lack of people skills—the ability to engage people and manage them effectively. One indicator God may be working through critics to get you to change is when several people are all critical about the same issue. Despite several voices speaking the same critical word, I was resistant to change. Explain, justify, and argue was my strategy to convince everyone in the parade they were out of step—but I was marching along just fine.

Then my mom came for a visit. At the time she wasn't an active church attendee. She went to church with us, however, heard me preach, watched me interact with people, and joined our family for lunch. During the meal she said, "Jeff, you are a good speaker. But if you don't learn how to work with people, you will never make it as a pastor."

How dare a person who had only been to my church once, who had limited experience observing church leaders, and who had never been a pastor or known the pressures of dealing with so many different personalities criticize me! What could my mom possibly know about my actions, motives, or skills in working with people after observing me only one Sunday? It was outrageous, ridiculous, frivolous, and pointless for her to have an opinion about my pastoral skills.

And yet, God's quiet voice whispered, "Your mom may be a casual observer, but isn't it interesting she is saying the same thing as people who work with you all the time? She knows you best, has known you longest, and only wants you to succeed. She has no other motive but your welfare. Pay attention, Jeff; there's something here for you to learn."

Even though her criticism stung, she was right. God was trying to get my attention about an important issue— working effectively with people. People were an expendable resource to be used for my success. That's painful to admit, but it was true. It took painful criticism to motivate needed life change. That criticism motivated me to improve my people skills, change my view of ministry relationships, and work with people in healthier ways. God used my critics to change me at the point of their criticism.

God will give you an opportunity to love your enemies.

Jesus said, "Love your enemies" (Matt. 5:44). That is more than a lofty ethic. It's a clear command coupled with a veiled promise. Since Jesus said to love your enemies, the subtle implication is: you are going to have some. That's a promise every leader knows has been fulfilled.

My election to my first denominational leadership role took place in a meeting with more than five hundred people present. The debate about my candidacy included several people who spoke against my election. One person, in particular, spoke against me with fervor. He had many reasons for opposing me and made an articulate case. Eventually I was elected, but not without it becoming clear this critic would continue to be suspicious of my leadership.

Two years passed. He phoned my office and asked for an immediate appointment about an urgent matter. I thought, "This can't be good" and braced for the worst. When he arrived, he told me about a tragic personal trial in his family and asked for my help. In that moment Jesus' instructions to love my enemies came to mind. My answer was yes, and we walked through the crisis together. Today my former critic is a friend. God allowed a critic to give me the opportunity to love someone who had hurt me. And through it, God gave me a friend. Sometimes loving an enemy changes a relationship. But always it changes us.

God shapes forbearance in you.

Having a persistent, consistent critic is particularly challenging. Some situations don't resolve themselves in weeks or months. Some of my most devoted critics have stayed on the job for years.

During my first pastorate, one woman disliked just about everything about me for years. How bad was it? When I saw her coming down a hall on a Sunday morning, I would duck into a classroom to "see someone about something." I wanted to avoid her acid tongue until after the worship service. Then after the service I would speak to her and her family and try my best to connect in a positive way. After about six years, a thaw occurred in our relationship through a crisis ministry to her daughter. A few weeks later I announced my resignation. She approached me in a huff and said, "I can't believe you're leaving. You've just now learned how to be my pastor." With that, she turned and walked away. That was our last and, sadly, best conversation over more than six years.

Another critic was a pastor who wrote, called, or personally communicated his opposition to my leadership decisions for almost a decade. After attempts to love him, conciliate him, confront him, and finally ignore him—the conclusion was simply to endure his persistent criticism. He wasn't changing his mind, so living with his infrequent but pointed barbs was the only option.

Another critic was equally persistent but much more aggressive. My unwillingness to respond favorably to his initial criticism escalated his attack. Many months and significant funds were spent answering his baseless complaints. It was personally and organizationally draining. Nothing seemed to mitigate the criticism as it dragged on and on. The critic finally went dormant, but no resolution was ever reached.

Through situations like these, God shapes an important character quality—forbearance—in us. Forbearance, a stronger word than patience but closely related, is one fruit of the Spirit (Gal. 5:22). It's a fruit that grows only under duress. To produce this fruit you need prolonged pressure, tension, or difficulty. God arranges those circumstances in a number of ways—through illness, personal crisis, ministry challenges, or through a persistent critic. Sometimes all you can do is endure and mature.

God allows you to share a small part of the sufferings of Jesus.

Our Lord was "reviled" (Matt. 27:39; Mark 15:32 KJV). The verbal assault he endured was the least of his sufferings, yet it probably wounded him emotionally and made him more vulnerable to the later physical blows. When a person is already verbally browbeaten, other kinds of attacks are even more painful.

Getting cussed out is never fun. While there are far worse forms of suffering, verbal abuse still hurts. God allows it to remind you how tepid your sufferings really are. When reviled, rather than feeling sorry for yourself, remember how mild your suffering is compared to what Jesus endured. Verbal abuse is "momentary light affliction" (2 Cor. 4:17) compared to Jesus' sufferings and that of Christian leaders in oppressed societies around the world.

Allow God and Others to Handle Your Critics

When Shimei attacked, David refused to silence the criticism. Even though Abishai was willing and able, David sensed God was somehow at work in the process and refused to avenge his attacker. David had some sense this wasn't the end of the story.

David soon regained his kingdom. He returned triumphantly to resume his throne, crossing the Jordan River with his entourage. And who was there to meet him? Shimei!

Shimei rushed to meet David and ferry his family and household belongings across the river (2 Sam. 19:16–23). When Shimei arrived, "he fell down before the king and said, to him, 'My lord, don't hold me guilty, and don't remember your servant's wrongdoing on the day my lord the king left Jerusalem. May the king not take it to heart. For your servant knows that I have sinned. But look! Today I am the first one of the entire house of Joseph to come down to meet my lord the king'" (2 Sam. 19:18–20).

Forgive my incredulity, but have you ever read a more pathetic, whining, sniveling statement? Shimei had changed his tune and was now ready to say and do anything to save his life. But Abishai saw through his duplicity and asked, "Shouldn't Shimei be put to death for this, because he ridiculed the LORD's anointed?" (2 Sam. 19:21). Good old Abishai! That's more like it.

But David was unwilling to take revenge on the day he reclaimed his throne. He replied, "'Should any man be killed in Israel today? Am I not aware that today I'm king over Israel?' So the king said to Shimei, 'You will not die'" (2 Sam. 19:22–23). David didn't need to destroy someone to establish his authority or restore his prestige. He gave his word Shimei wouldn't die that day. But that's not the end of the story.

Several years later David was dying. He was consolidating his kingdom and preparing to make the transfer to Solomon. As he lay on his deathbed, he summoned his son to give him final instructions. His last words were profound. He told Solomon, "'Keep an eye on Shimei. . . . He uttered malicious curses against me the day I went to Mahanaim. But he came down to meet me at the Jordan River, and I swore to him by the LORD: "I will never kill you with the sword." So don't let him go unpunished, for you are a wise man. You know how to deal with him to bring his gray head down to Sheol with blood.' Then David rested with his fathers" (1 Kings 2:8–10).

While David had spared Shimei's life, he hadn't forgotten his attack or his duplicity at the Jordan River crossing. While David hadn't killed Shimei to exact revenge or establish his kingdom, neither did he completely trust him. With his last breath, he warned Solomon to watch Shimei and find a way to hold him accountable.

As Solomon took steps to establish his reign, he summoned Shimei for a meeting early in his tenure as king (1 Kings 2:36–46). He told Shimei, "Build a house for yourself in Jerusalem and live there, but don't leave there and go anywhere else. On the day you do leave and cross the Kidron Valley, know for sure that you will certainly die. Your blood will be on your own head" (vv. 36–37). Solomon placed Shimei under "house arrest"—allowing him to build a house and live in Jerusalem but not leave the city. This was a brilliant solution. Solomon could watch a potential enemy, while at the same time allowing him to determine his fate.

Shimei responded with the same effusive, dubious support for Solomon he had previously given David. He replied, "'The sentence is fair; your servant will do as my lord the king has spoken.' And Shimei lived in Jerusalem for a long time" (v. 38).

But not long enough. After three years, two of Shimei's slaves ran away. He left Jerusalem, retrieved them from Gath, and returned home. When Solomon learned of his disobedience, he summoned him.

> "Didn't I make you swear by the LORD and warn you, saying, 'On the day you leave and go anywhere else, know for sure that you will certainly die'? And you said to me, 'The sentence is fair; I will obey.' So why have you not kept the LORD's oath and the command that I gave you? . . . You yourself know all the evil that you did to my father David. Therefore, the LORD has brought back your evil on your head, but King Solomon will be blessed, and David's throne will remain established before the LORD forever."
>
> Then the king commanded Benaiah son of Jehoiada, and he went out and struck Shimei down, and he died. So the kingdom was established in Solomon's hands. (1 Kings 2:42–46)

Ah, the wisdom of Solomon! He handled this critic perfectly. He gave him clear boundaries and allowed him to discredit himself. He avoided revenge but enforced accountability. Solomon kept his focus on what Shimei had done to him, not what he had done to his father. In doing so, he avoided the leader's dilemma of wrongly taking action based on offenses against a friend or family member. He also kept the focus on Shimei's actions of leaving Jerusalem—definable, public, and documented—in violation of their agreement.

It's difficult, if not impossible, to adequately address or handle some critics. You must trust God and others to make things right. Remember my wife's critic mentioned in the previous chapter? After a few years, God orchestrated an interesting turn of events. The critic's husband became a pastor. Within a few months, we received another letter. We almost threw it away without opening it, afraid it would only bring more discouraging criticism. But we were quite surprised. The critic had become the object of criticism. As a pastor's wife, she was now seeing the situation from the inside and had critics hounding her. The letter was an apology to Ann for the past criticisms. Ann was able to make contact and bring positive closure—and offer encouragement—in a previously strained relationship.

Watching God discipline critics is painful. There's no joy in seeing another person suffer, even when she has hurt you. God has ways of protecting you—after he accomplishes his purpose through your critic—to limit the damage in your life. Sometimes, though, it seems critics are getting away with their actions. And, in the short run of this lifetime, it may actually turn out that way. But remember, "God is not mocked. For whatever a man sows he will also reap" (Gal. 6:7). And also remember, all will appear before "God and Christ Jesus, who is going to judge the living and the dead" (2 Tim. 4:1).

You can trust God to hold your critics accountable. He may discipline your critics in this life or judge them in the next, but everyone who attacks you unjustly will be held accountable. Trust God to make things right—in his time, in his way, without your plotting retribution or taking revenge.

Conclusion

When critics attack us, we are the object of the conflict. But what do you do when your followers are in conflict with each other? Are you simply an innocent bystander? Are you responsible to intervene? Should you leave others to work out their own problems? Followers in conflict create pain for ministry leaders. While we can't assure harmony, we can learn to manage our response to conflict to minimize personal and organizational damage. Toward that end, we turn our attention in the next chapter.

9

Managing Followers in Conflict

Quarreling followers drain energy from ministry leaders. Their bickering and its collateral damage can take an emotional, spiritual, and even physical toll on you. Learning to manage conflict situations you didn't cause and can't control is a delicate balance of organizational responsibilities (including legal issues with employees) and interpersonal dynamics. It can be made even more complicated by your friendships with followers. This is a common situation among Christian leaders and followers who share unity in Jesus Christ and often consider their relationship more than a professional affiliation. Managing followers in conflict is a complex challenge.

You may question my matter-of-fact assumption that conflict occurs among believers in Christian organizations. Admitting conflict exists doesn't condone it or justify it. But dealing with reality is one of the themes of this book.

Your followers will, from time to time, have conflict with each other. People have been in conflict since sin entered the world just after creation. Christians have been having conflict with each other since the earliest days of the church. Let's take a look at some of those early conflicts along with contemporary examples in churches and Christian ministries today to gain some perspective on handling this problem.

Kinds of Conflicts Leaders Face

Church members have conflict.

This isn't a new phenomenon. Two women in the first-century church at Philippi struggled to get along. Paul wrote, "So then, in this way, my dearly loved brothers, my joy and crown, stand firm in the Lord, dear friends. I urge Euodia and I urge Syntyche to agree in the Lord. Yes, I also ask you, true partner, to help these women who have contended for the gospel at my side" (Phil. 4:1–3).

What can we learn from this brief reference to these two feuding women? First, they were having significant conflict. Paul often mentioned individuals in his letters but usually in a positive light. When he mentioned a problem or shortcoming, it was usually in a person's relationship with God or with him. But this time, he wrote about two women in conflict with each other. It must have been a significant conflict for the news to reach Paul in Rome. The importance of resolving it required specific mention in an open letter read to the church. These women were having serious, public, church-impacting conflict.

Second, their hope for resolving the conflict was to

"agree in the Lord." Paul reminded them of their common relationship with Jesus and the potential for unity in him. That was, after all, their only hope of unity (and ours as well). Third, these women were committed Christians with a demonstrated effectiveness in sharing the gospel. Paul considered them coworkers who had "contended for the gospel at my side." This is an important insight. We often incorrectly assume carnal, shallow, or immature believers are the only ones who have conflict. But in this case, it was two prominent and effective gospel workers who were at odds. Finally, church leaders had some responsibility to "help these women" resolve their conflict. While instructions on how to do this aren't specified, other biblical passages help us know how to navigate these troubled waters. We will consider some of those strategies later.

While we don't know the nature of the conflict between Euodia and Syntyche, it might have been something like this. A pastor called the Monday after Easter for counsel on a conflict that erupted between two women in his church just before the Easter morning worship service. One woman directed the choir. The other woman directed the Sunday school. Because the choir had a major Easter musical program to present, the director instructed choir members to leave their Sunday school classes fifteen minutes early to prepare for the presentation. This wasn't a large church so the exodus from the three adult classes was noticeable and distracting. The Sunday school director wasn't pleased since the Sunday school had many guests that day. She erupted in anger, loudly confronting the choir director on the sanctuary platform just prior to the beginning of the worship service. It was a mess! The pastor was shocked, the choir devastated, and the Easter morning crowd astounded as these two women shouted at each other in front of everyone.

This incident was the culmination of a long, simmering conflict between these two women. The pressure of Easter Sunday (both on the choir for its program and on the Sunday school for its enlarged attendance) caused the conflict to become public. The timing could not have been worse. A large crowd went home that Sunday with a special Easter memory—something never before seen in this church—two out-of-control middle-aged women having a verbal cat fight!

To be fair, men have the same kind of conflicts. One church had many men who were union members, as well as a few managers. These two groups often approached church problems as if they were negotiating an employment contract. The pastor observed when a committee, work group, or class consisted of only union men, they functioned with reasonable harmony. They understood and trusted each other. But when the managers were put into the mix, it was always much more difficult to reach consensus. Trust was lower, dialogue truncated, and decisions took much longer because of the underlying tension in their extrachurch relationships. Occasionally this tension erupted in angry or terse exchanges over seemingly minor problems.

Church members, particularly in smaller churches, consider themselves one, big happy family. What they mean by this is unity and cordiality mark their relationships. But have you considered how real families relate? Most extended families have sibling rivalry, tension with in-laws, troublesome cousins, meddlesome aunts or uncles, and simmering conflict between any or all of these groups. So church is like family after all—but not in the ways we typically imply when we call the church the "family of God."

Church members, no matter how committed they are to the Lord or how skilled you are as a leader, will occasionally have conflict. It's inevitable. Denying it is unhealthy; ignoring it can be lethal to your long-term effectiveness. Church leaders must have realistic expectations about their followers and strategies in place to manage conflicts among them.

Employees have conflict.

Ministry organizations like schools, mission boards, and parachurch organizations have employees instead of members. It's difficult to find biblical examples of these relationships because ministry organizations didn't exist then in the same forms they do today. Ministry employees were not a common concept in the first-century church.

There are biblical examples, however, of conflict between people in comparable roles. For instance, David and Joab had conflict (a king in conflict with a general) over Joab's killing of Abner and Amasa, David's response to Absalom's death, David's census of the army, and David's complicity in Uriah's murder. Jesus had to deal with dissension among his disciples, for example, James and John asking to sit at his right hand. Many of the realities outlined in the previous section about church members also apply to ministry employees. They are committed Christians who, despite their best intentions, still have conflicts with peers and supervisors.

Two long-term employees had a growing tension because of several incidents that fueled their frustrations over time. Their relationship finally became toxic, so troublesome it seemed that someone had to be found in the wrong and be terminated. But in this case, their supervisor negotiated a job change and departmental transfer for one of the employees (to create a cooling-off period). Within days, the tension evaporated and both employees began to work in much more productive ways. The residual damage to the organization as other employees worked through their response to the solution was still problematic but also eventually was resolved.

In another instance, a supervisor became abusive to a certain employee—singling her out with negative comments, public criticism, and demeaning assignments. She complained to a manager who intervened to discover the scope and cause of the conflict. Unfortunately a pattern of abuse out of character for the supervisor, but nonetheless evident, was discovered. He was terminated. The situation was ripe for potential litigation (for sexual harassment and gender bias). It was prevented only by the manager's intentional intervention and the employee's willingness to allow the termination to end the matter.

In another case, a supervisor told an employee to lie to the organization about an employment matter. When she refused, these two employees had conflict, which escalated as others learned about the situation. The supervisor claimed he had been misunderstood. The employee maintained she had been put in an untenable position—told to lie to continue her employment. Eventually this situation was resolved by the departure of the supervisor.

These situations illustrate the kinds of conflicts among employees and between employees and supervisors in Christian organizations. Christian employees struggle with interpersonal relationships. Christian supervisors make serious mistakes in how they relate to employees. Otherwise solid employees and supervisors make decisions incongruous with their past character and performance. In short, people make mistakes, and those mistakes sometimes damage relationships in organizations. This kind of unacceptable behavior has to be confronted. It's an unpleasant responsibility, but people may lose jobs, be transferred, or be disciplined to rectify unacceptable behavior.

Must it be this way in Christian organizations? My answer may surprise you: *Yes*. Christian organizations usually have fewer personnel problems than secular organizations, but they still employ people—sinful, imperfect people. So while Christian organizations have fewer personnel conflicts, they should still expect them. Just as you should expect conflict among church members, you should expect conflict among Christian employees and have strategies in place to manage those conflicts.

Leadership teams have conflict.

Even the most committed Christians and most prominent leaders will occasionally have conflict. Two biblical examples demonstrate how old this problem is. Paul and Barnabas were the dynamic duo of the early church and early missionary movement. They first worked together in Antioch (Acts 11:19–30) and were sent by that church on the first missionary journey (Acts 13:3). They worked well together and God blessed their efforts. When they started their work, Barnabas was the team leader (based on his early leadership in Antioch). Barnabas is mentioned first in Acts when he and Paul began their missionary work. Soon, however, Paul became the more prominent team member and was recognized as the spokesman and leader.

In Acts 15:36–41, after partnering for years from the founding of the church at Antioch through the Jerusalem Council, Paul and Barnabas were preparing for their second missionary journey. While doing so, they had a major conflict. John Mark, Barnabas's nephew, had previously "deserted them in Pamphylia and had not gone on with them to the work" (v. 38). Barnabas wanted to give Mark another chance. Paul adamantly refused. These two godly, spiritually dynamic leaders had "such a sharp disagreement that they parted company" (v. 39). They argued vehemently and decided they could no longer work together in the ministry. Another team member, Silas, was drawn into the conflict. Paul chose him as his new partner, leaving Barnabas and Mark to form another missionary team and go their separate ways (vv. 39–40). The Antioch church was also drawn into the conflict. Paul and Silas "departed, after being commended to the grace of the Lord by the brothers" (v. 40). No blessing by the Antioch church on the Barnabas/Mark team is recorded. That's a pointed omission. The church apparently made a judgment on the conflict's results by extending its blessing exclusively to Paul and Silas. Given Barnabas's storied history as the pastoral leader in Antioch, this is a stunning omission and conclusion.

Paul was also part of a serious conflict with another leadership peer. Peter made a wrong decision regarding fellowship with Gentiles in the face of Jewish pressure to limit his contact with uncircumcised believers, thus compromising the nature of the gospel (Gal. 2:12–14). Paul "opposed him to his face" (v. 11) and told Peter "in front of everyone, 'If you, who are a Jew, live like a Gentile and not like a Jew, how can you compel Gentiles to live like Jews?'" (v. 14). Sorting out the theological issues and implications addressed in this conflict is not germane for our purposes. This key point in the story is important: Christian leaders—even the most committed, gifted, and highly placed leaders—sometimes have significant conflict. These conflicts can be serious (about issues like the nature of the gospel), personal (involving direct confrontation), and public (in front of the church, including the church at large these days through the media).

Ministry leadership teams have conflict. Team members—like Paul, Barnabas, Mark, and Silas—had conflict with and among each other. Paul and Peter, the two heavyweights of the first-century church, had an open, intense conflict. These examples demonstrate the reality of conflict among leaders. No matter how spiritual and committed your leadership team members, they are still susceptible to conflict.

My experience parallels these biblical examples. Over the years I have worked with outstanding team members in church, denominational, and seminary leadership. They have honored me with their loyalty, commitment to a shared vision, and willingness to sacrifice together to advance our mission. Yet, in spite of sterling character and unquestioned commitment, conflict has occasionally happened among them. Team members have divided over personalities, strategies, doctrine, and personnel choices. Sometimes those conflicts were part of making good decisions as we wrestled with options. But other times, the conflicts have been more divisive and revealed serious rifts in relationships. In those cases, intervention has been required and sometimes team members have had to be replaced.

Conflict among your leadership team is inevitable. Denying this reality isn't healthy and will only exacerbate the problem when it happens. Developing intentional strategies to manage these conflicts is a better option. Let's turn our attention to developing strategies to respond to followers in conflict. Remember the focus of this chapter is on helping you, as a leader, to manage your response to followers in conflict. It isn't about preventing conflict, but on strategies for managing your response to conflict when it happens among your members, followers, or leadership team. Doing this well will minimize the pain of making hard decisions about your closest associates.

Anticipate Problems

Good leaders deal with reality, not wishful thinking about how things ought to be or how we hope they will be. When it comes to conflict among followers—expect it. This doesn't mean you are negative or pessimistic about people. It simply means you are realistic about the dynamics of human relationships in organizations—including churches and ministries. People will occasionally get cross with each other. It's inevitable. When you accept this reality, it will help you handle your response, particularly your emotional responses.

Anger is a common reaction when faced with followers in conflict. It's easy to become angry because of lost time you devote to the problem, lost productivity if they are employees, and damage the conflict causes as other people choose sides or are otherwise impacted. But your anger is counterproductive because "man's anger does not accomplish God's righteousness" (James 1:20). Preparing to manage conflict as an inevitable part of your leadership role will lessen your anger when conflict erupts.

Anxiety is another common reaction. As a young leader, my blood pressure skyrocketed whenever anyone around me was in conflict. I wrongly assumed any conflict was a sign of poor leadership on my part. My insecurities kept me on edge lest the conflict be blamed on me and supposedly weaken my leadership. During those early years of working with followers in conflict, my typical response was intensive intervention to smooth over every conflict as rapidly as possible. My motive was relieving my anxiety about the situation, not guiding people through a healthy process of resolving their issues. That strategy seldom worked.

Instead of anger or anxiety, respond to followers in conflict with patience, poise, and peace. A measured, deliberate response has a remarkable effect on conflict situations. It defuses intensity and helps people gain fresh perspective. It slows people down and allows them to think more clearly. It sets the stage for conflict resolution, not just soothing hurt feelings. Conflict among followers prompts a leader to pray, not worry, with peace as the result. This process is outlined just after the encouragement to resolve the conflict between Euodia and Syntyche. Paul prescribed, "Don't worry about anything, . . . let your requests be made known to God. And the peace of God, which surpasses every thought, will guard your hearts and your minds in Christ Jesus" (Phil. 4:6–7).

Being angry or anxious isn't helpful when working with people in conflict. A quiet peace creates an atmosphere more conducive to focusing on the true problems and working toward helpful solutions. Accept the reality that conflict management among church members or teammates is a part of your role. Develop the spiritual asset of a peaceful spirit in the face of conflict. It will enable you to effectively manage your relationship to followers in conflict and set the stage for the following steps toward a positive resolution.

Facilitate Appropriate Confrontation

Probably the most frequently used passage in the Bible on conflict resolution is: "'If your brother sins against you, go and rebuke him in private. If he listens to you, you have won your brother. But if he won't listen, take one or two more with you, so that by the testimony of two or three witnesses every fact may be established. If he pays no attention to them, tell the church. But if he doesn't pay attention even to the church, let him be like an unbeliever and a tax collector to you'" (Matt. 18:15–17).

Commentators have written extensively about the meaning of these verses and how to implement them in various conflict situations. For our purposes, let's draw some key insights from the passage. As you can easily see, both in the text and in the summary below, as conflict escalates in intensity, your attempts at resolution escalate correspondingly. Here then, are four key principles for responding to followers in conflict:

1. When a follower has a relational conflict, he or she must work it out with the other person.
2. When followers can't work out the conflict using principle 1, they should involve a small number of appropriate people to help resolve the conflict.
3. When followers can't work out a conflict using principles 1 or 2, they should then (and only then)

take the problem to a higher authority (a supervisor or pastor).

4. When a conflict can't be resolved, definitive action by appropriate authority to end the conflict is in order.

When a follower reports a conflict with a fellow church member, fellow employee, or supervisor, the first questions to ask are, "Have you talked with the person about this conflict, and what are the two of you doing to resolve it?" In a number of instances, people have told me, "No, I wanted to talk to you first." This is an attempt to turn their problem into my problem—practicing the time-honored management principle of trying to put their monkey on my back. Don't let this happen to you! The first step in conflict resolution among Christians—including among church members and employees—is direct conversation between the parties affected by the problem. Doing this allows both parties to state issues, clarify misunderstandings, extend apologies, offer and receive forgiveness, and solve problems before they become unmanageable. When a person comes to you with a conflict and he hasn't spoken to the other party, your response is simple—send him to the other party and stay out of it.

But what do you do when a follower comes to you after speaking to the other person, without achieving resolution? You direct her to apply the second principle. Encourage her to involve a small number of appropriate people in attempting to resolve the situation. And even though she has come to you, you aren't obligated to be in that small group of appropriate people. Particularly, if you are a senior pastor or senior leader in an organization, be careful not to become involved in the conflict resolution process prematurely. For church members, suggest they involve a trusted elder, deacon, or other leader or mature friend who knows both parties and can facilitate reconciliation. For employees, insist persons in conflict work with their immediate supervisor to resolve the problem. In either example, the biblical principle is being applied. When your followers aren't able to resolve a conflict face-to-face, they should seek help from appropriate persons in their church or organization who have the wisdom, maturity, and influence to bring about a workable solution.

The danger senior leaders fear at this point is that followers may indiscriminately spread their conflict by involving people who aren't part of the problem or potential solution. While taking this risk can potentially create another set of problems, it's still a risk worth taking. Most believers don't want to sow discord and will work to implement a process they hope will solve their conflict. Don't allow concern about how this process might be misused to keep you from implementing these biblical steps. While no method is foolproof when working with people, a good-faith attempt to apply biblical principles in conflict resolution will most likely produce healthy results.

But when conflict can't be resolved through individual meetings or by other believers intervening appropriately, the conflict has to be resolved by a higher authority. In a ministry organization, the highest authority is usually vested in the executive officers or governing board. Earlier, my counsel was to avoid involving yourself (as a senior leader) prematurely in conflict resolution. One reason for this is, you personify and represent the authority of your organization. For example, as a senior pastor, you represent your church and would be the person to bring a conflict situation before the church. As an executive leader, you would either be the final authority or would be the person to bring a conflict to an administrative council or governing board. In either case, you must avoid escalating a conflict to this level too rapidly. Most conflicts can and will be resolved by applying the first two reconciliation principles. Only those situations that have thoroughly exhausted the options at lower levels should come to you for resolution. Part of your leadership role is deflecting attempts by your followers to involve you prematurely in solving their conflicts.

This is so important because when a conflict comes to a senior leader, a church, or a governing board for ultimate resolution, the consequences can be (and usually are) severe. When a conflict reaches this level for resolution, church members may be disciplined (including being removed from membership) and employees may be reprimanded, demoted, penalized financially, or terminated. Be careful not to allow molehill-sized problems to be prematurely addressed with mountain-sized solutions. Don't shoot a mosquito with a howitzer! Press people to resolve conflict quickly, in less public venues, before this kind of final intervention is needed.

When a conflict finally comes to you for resolution, have the courage to take definitive action. When a church member must be removed, do it. While it will be painful in the short run, it will benefit the church in the long run. When an employee must be disciplined, do it. A friend once said, "You can't lead if you can't inflict pain." You may recoil from that statement, but it's true. There are times a leader must take definitive action to resolve relational conflict, stop inappropriate behavior, remove a person with an uncompromising or unforgiving spirit, or take other drastic action to end relational conflict and move a church or ministry organization forward. That's a painful process, but healers must often inflict temporary pain. Injections prevent disease, surgery removes cancer, and stitches close wounds but leave scars. These treatments are painful but necessary for long-term health. When the ultimate disciplinary action—termination—must be taken, it can be particularly painful. So much so that we will devote the entire next chapter to handling the difficult process of terminating people from your team.

Minimize Collateral Damage

An additional contribution you can make to the recovery process is to minimize the continuing damage the conflict may be causing in your church or organization. Again, it's important to have realistic expectations. Conflict, particularly open conflict that reaches such a critical phase it requires public resolution, will almost always have some negative impact. You can't stop this from happening, but, as a leader, you are uniquely positioned to limit the damage.

First, communicate the essential facts supporting your decision to resolve the conflict (why you are disciplining or removing members from your church, demoting or terminating employees from your organization, etc.). After that, say as little as possible about the situation to as few people as possible. When your decision is final and implemented, stop talking about it. Stop talking about it, period. Your followers, including those on your leadership team, assume what you talk about is what is important to you. So change the subject. If a conflict was resolved before it reached you, it may still have negative impact in a smaller sphere of influence. Even in these situations, it's important to help followers limit conversation about the past and move on.

Second, hold other followers accountable for their reaction to the conflict (and any decision you made to resolve it). If gossip erupts, confront it. If murmuring begins, stop it. If employees protest, hear their concerns but reinforce your decision. Be discerning and patient. Don't engage in unnecessary conflict with people who initially react emotionally to your decision. Those reactions should be expected and tolerated. They usually dissipate quickly. But be firm in confronting persistent complaints. And again, if the conflict was resolved personally or with the assistance of a small group of trusted confidants, these same principles apply. Hold people accountable for their response to conflict *and* to resolved conflict.

Third, refocus the church, organization, department, class, or program on its purpose or mission. Every church or ministry organization has an overarching mission. Every program, department, or class of a church or organization also has a role in fulfilling the mission of the whole. To aid in moving on from a past conflict, help church members or employees refocus on their mission, their purpose, their role. Get them busy working on common tasks, working toward common goals, and focusing on the future. Doing this helps people put lesser issues in perspective.

Finally, if you are struggling to work through residual pain, guilt, disappointment, or other heartache caused by the situation, discuss it with someone outside your church or organization (like your wise guys). Continuing to talk about it, even among your closest leadership circle, will only prolong the process of your church or organization truly moving forward. You may very well need to talk through the issues to finalize your feelings about its resolution. Just don't do it within your team. And do your spouse a favor and don't rehearse or rehash the problem at home. If you need to talk it out, turn to a mentor, peer in another church or organization, denominational leader, or other friend in ministry leadership.

Conclusion

Managing followers in conflict isn't easy, but it's a required skill for Christian leaders. While we optimistically hope our followers will always exhibit Christian grace and unity in relationships, we recognize this won't always be the case. Even our most trusted followers and most mature partners can succumb to baser desires that harm relationships. Preparing to cope with followers in conflict isn't a concession to diminished expectations in your church or organization. It is, instead, a practical strategy for shepherding people under our leadership during times of unseemly, unsettling behavior. Wise leaders prepare for the worst behavior among their followers, while never losing confidence in their capacity for the best.

Unfortunately, as already mentioned, sometimes conflict leads to terminating a person from your team. No one enjoys this part of senior leadership, but if you lead for a while, this delicate responsibility will eventually fall to you. And it will probably be painful. So continue reading for insight into this unseemly but necessary part of a leader's responsibility.

10

Terminating Someone from Your Team

Y ou're fired" is Donald Trump's famous tagline on his television show *The Apprentice*. While the pseudosuspense of a reality show can be entertaining, actually sitting across a desk from a colleague and saying the same words is no joking matter. For many Christian leaders, the most difficult words they can imagine saying to a team member are, "You're fired." We go to great lengths, sometimes to the detriment of our organizations, our missions, our other followers, and even to the person being terminated, to avoid saying those two potent words. But if you lead any size church or ministry organization, even if your workers are all volunteers, you will eventually need to terminate a team member. Given this inevitability, it's essential to understand some principles about how and when to terminate someone appropriately. This won't alleviate all painful aspects of this leadership dilemma, but it will give you resources and skills to manage yourself in these situations. Hopefully, the result will be a less painful experience both for you and the terminated person.

If you lead a smaller church or organization, you may be tempted to stop reading since you don't have a large number of employees (or perhaps any employees!). But you still have supervisory responsibility, even if your team members are all volunteers. Volunteers often have more nebulous job descriptions and expectations. Their terms of service and expected tenure are also less defined. For these reasons, it can be more difficult to remove a volunteer from a ministry role than to terminate an employee. Many principles in this chapter apply equally whether you are dealing with employees or volunteers. So keep reading, because no matter the number or type of people you supervise, sooner or later, you will need to terminate, dismiss, or reassign someone on your team.

Why Terminations Are Difficult

Terminations are difficult for Christian leaders for several reasons. Christian leaders (particularly pastors) are redemptive people who feel they can "save" everyone. If we invest enough time, offer enough prayer, and provide enough training and support, we are convinced we can help anyone succeed. We believe we can teach, train, or coach any willing follower to fulfill an assigned role. It's difficult to admit when we can't change a person, or even help him change, and must remove him from our team.

I once devoted a year shaping a lay leader for a ministry position. He wanted the job, was willing to meet with me often for training, and tried his best. He responded well to my instruction and correction, in the moment. But then he would make the same mistakes, over and over, as if we had never talked. Finally I had to tell him he could no longer serve in his current leadership capacity. It was a difficult conversation. I knew he would be disappointed and might leave our church. But it was also difficult because I had to admit my inability to coach him to improvement. This was compounded because I had asked him to assume the position in the first place. So one reason you may have trouble terminating someone is your belief that you can "fix" anyone—if you just give the person more time, training, and support.

Another reason we are reluctant to terminate someone, unique to Christian leaders, is our respect for God's call and our claims of discerning God's direction. When we place someone in a leadership role, we often speak of God "calling" the person and our sense of God's direction in the process. A logical question is, "If God calls a person to a role, how can he or she later be inadequate for it and have to be *uncalled?*" Another difficult question is, "If God directed you to choose a person, what has changed to allow you to terminate him or her from your team?" Except in cases of moral or ethical misconduct, these are difficult questions to answer. It's hard to admit a mistake in choosing a person or placing him in a leadership role. It's also hard for the person being terminated to accept that his job requirements may have changed since his selection and he no longer fits the organization's needs. No matter the reason for the termination, it's difficult to take action we feel might be contradicting God's call or clashing with God's direction. Sorting this out requires discernment.

Christian leaders also have a hard time terminating someone because we don't like confrontation. We want people to like us. We don't want to disappoint people. For these reasons, we delay confronting underperforming volunteers and employees. We couch this in spiritual terms like, "I'm praying about it." What we are really praying is for God to get us off the hook by telling the person to quit! That seldom works, by the way. Delay strategies also include secretly hoping a struggling person will do something really bad so the termination will be clearly justified, thus minimizing potential conflict with remaining personnel. That seldom works either. I know these strategies don't work. I've tried them!

Fear of confrontation, even when required by an employee's extended pattern of poor performance, may cause you to delay taking action or to take inappropriate action. Duplicity and delay in these matters often results in a worse confrontation than would have occurred had you handled the problem in a timely manner. The whole matter may become more painful than an appropriate, earlier confrontation would have produced.

We also don't like terminating people because it can be costly. Terminating an employee takes an emotional toll on you as a leader. But it can also cost you time devoted to developing the termination plan, reorganizing to cover the tasks formerly done by the terminated person (also taking time from other people), time and money spent searching for a new person, and financial costs associated with the termination (like severance pay and benefits or the cost of a temporary employee to cover necessary tasks). Terminations can be costly. They can take an emotional and financial toll, as well as burn up time we could have devoted to other tasks. As we will see later in the chapter, however, sometimes *not* terminating a person can be even more costly.

Finally, Christian leaders struggle with terminations because the people we work with are friends and colleagues—brothers and sisters in Jesus Christ. We share a spiritual bond. As Christian leaders, we are obligated to behave ethically toward all people, especially fellow believers we supervise. Whether our team members are employees or volunteers, we consider them like family and feel responsible for their well-being. Creating pain, disappointment, and hardship by terminating one of them isn't easy—even when we believe it's best for the person and the organization in the long run. Christian leaders are, after all, *Christian* leaders. We are supposed to be models of ethical leadership. We are supposed to care for people as Jesus did. That's challenging when our responsibility for the good of our organization rubs against our personal relationship with any individual employee. Keeping your organization's mission, the good of the many, and the potential for long-term positive results for the terminated person in view will help you make compassionate termination decisions.

For all these reasons, and others you might add, it's painful to remove employees or volunteers from a ministry position. But while it's hard for Christian leaders to terminate team members, sometimes it must be done. There are good reasons—related to the overall goals of accomplishing God's mission through your organization and healthy spiritual supervision of personnel—that mandate these tough decisions.

When to Terminate Someone

Termination is the best and only ethical decision in some situations. The easiest termination decision is when a person makes a deliberate choice that compromises his integrity. This may surprise you, but the easiest terminations are those involving immorality, financial mismanagement, or gross insubordination. Most people assume these decisions are gut wrenching and may comfort you or commiserate with you. But they really aren't that difficult. While the circumstances causing the termination are painful, the actual decision to terminate the person isn't too complicated. In these situations, there's no other legitimate option but termination. Any other response compromises your integrity as a leader and disillusions your other followers. While the circumstances surrounding the termination may be troubling, the decision to terminate a person engaged in these actions isn't difficult. A serious breach of moral or ethical standards calls for a swift, definitive response.

Terminating a person for inadequate job performance is more difficult. These situations are more subjective, require more careful analysis and documentation, and are largely based on your judgment of the person's performance. While it may be clear to you, as you will discover, your conclusions won't always be as clear to the terminated person or other people in your organization. Still, one of the reasons to remove a person from a position is she simply doesn't have the skills necessary to do the job. You may struggle with this kind of termination because you second-guess yourself on determining her competency. You may also resist because you don't want to be perceived as judgmental, uncaring, or heavy-handed. But, as a leader, you are ultimately responsible for your organization's health, not each person's individual happiness. Organizational performance is determined by the collective performance of individuals; therefore, analyzing individual performance is essential for improving organizational effectiveness. Evaluating volunteers and employees, placing them in appropriate positions, helping them develop necessary skills, motivating them to excellence, disciplining them when required, and removing them when necessary is part of your job as a leader.

How does a person end up in a position for which he isn't qualified and from which he must be terminated? Sometimes it's through poor placement practices. When you rush to place someone just to fill a gap (like asking the wrong person to lead a Sunday school class), you can wind up later having to remove the same person. It can also happen when a person's skills deteriorate (sometimes through no fault of his own). One administrative assistant became less and less capable over time. She lost the ability to remember details, maintain her assigned work schedule, and learn new skills as the organization changed. Eventually she had to be replaced. It can also happen when job expectations change. An executive assistant's boss retired. Her new boss was much younger. She had a tough time adjusting to his greater use of technology and faster-paced work style. She also had to be replaced. Sometimes a person is placed in the wrong job. Sometimes a person's skills deteriorate. Sometimes the expectations of the job change. In all these cases, poor performance can result in an employee needing to be reassigned or replaced.

Some team members can also lose interest in their work, stop producing necessary results, or be otherwise deficient in their duties. Both volunteers and employees, if they don't respond to correction or further training, must be dismissed when any of these circumstances can't be resolved. Prolonged poor employee performance rightly leads to termination.

Another reason for termination, or perhaps reassignment, is when a person is in the wrong job. This could be because he's the wrong person in the right job or might be the right person in the wrong job. While one volunteer youth leader was passionate about teenagers learning to follow God, both his personality and ministry approach were more suited to working with adults. He was too impatient to effectively reach teenagers. But, with adults, his expectations were more realistic. He didn't need to be dismissed; he needed to be reassigned.

Another example of a person being in the wrong job was moving an educator into an administrator's role. Since she was such a good teacher, it was assumed she would be good administering an educational program. Wrong! She was unhappy and unproductive in her new role. She was still the right person but in the wrong job. When she moved back to teaching, she again flourished—as did her students. A common analogy, made famous in *Good to Great* by Jim Collins, equates staffing decisions to a bus trip. The challenge for leaders is to get the right people on the bus, and then get them in the right seats on the bus. In other words, get the right people on your team and then be sure they are assigned the most suitable job to benefit the organization. Assigning team members their role is your responsibility. Termination may be required if a person simply doesn't belong on your bus. Removing him from the bus, however, doesn't mean you have to throw him under the bus! You serve some people best by helping them find the bus where their skills are needed and will be appreciated. Doing this in a healthy way will be covered later in this chapter.

Organizational change, particularly changes in senior

leadership, also creates the potential need to replace or reassign team members. This situation is sometimes part of a new senior pastor arriving at a church, a new senior leader coming to an organization, or even a new senior leader in a division or department. It's usually wise, however, to resist making wholesale changes and work with inherited team members until you accurately appraise their gifts and suitability for your future plans. Then you can find meaningful ways for them to contribute to your organization's future or help them leave in a mutually acceptable way. The slash-and-burn method of organizational change is almost never in the long-term best interest of any ministry organization. It's much better to take your time to discover the talents of your inherited team members, and if possible, assign them to new roles more compatible to your leadership style, their giftedness, and the changing nature of your organization. But if that's not possible, mutual separation or termination may still be necessary.

Results of Terminating Someone

When termination or reassignment is necessary, the ramifications of the personnel change must be managed. You need a transition plan to address intended consequences and wisdom to respond to unintended consequences. The transition plan should outline termination protocol, steps to replace the terminated person, and how to manage in the meantime. But despite good planning, how a termination unfolds can't be predicted or controlled. There are collateral results you may experience when you terminate or reassign someone on your team. Some of those results may pleasantly surprise you. Others may be an unavoidable part of the painful side of leadership. Here is a sample of the kind of results you may experience.

When an employee or a volunteer is removed from a job, she is free to find a position more suited to her skills and interests. While termination is often painful in the short run, it can be a blessing in disguise for the terminated person. If your judgment is accurate about a lack of suitability for her former position, she may even feel liberated. One employee, after being reassigned to a different position, thanked his supervisor. He was frustrated in his former position and was delighted to have an opportunity to have a new job without having to leave his organization or relocate his family. He accepted his new position and thrived as a long-term employee in a different role more suited to his strengths. Some terminations are not adversarial and turn into a growth opportunity for the displaced person.

Terminations, and the situations leading to them, have impact on others in your ministry organization. When you tolerate an ineffective employee, unwilling to reassign or terminate him, it demoralizes others on your team. Sometimes leaders delay terminating a problem employee or volunteer because of concerns about how others on the team will respond. But often, when a termination has been clearly justified by poor performance, other employees are grateful for the change. On occasion, team members will quietly communicate gratitude to you for making the hard call to replace an ineffective person. This has happened to me after replacing both employees and volunteers. People know when they are working with or for an ineffective person. They want to be on a high-performance team or in a high-performance organization. When someone limits their effectiveness by poor performance, both employees and volunteers want someone to do something. And that someone is you! Don't be afraid team members will be angry or a justified personnel change will demoralize your crew. Usually the opposite will happen as both team performance and morale often improve after this kind of termination.

When you terminate an ineffective person, mutiny by the remaining crew seldom happens. Your worst fears rarely materialize. A church had a worship leader who was underperforming. After six months of regular meetings to supervise, coach, and counsel him about needed areas of improvement, his performance was still inadequate. He was dismissed. The pastor feared an exodus from the worship team, and perhaps the church. The opposite happened. The week following the termination, the worship team met to create the following Sunday's worship service. Two people in the congregation, who had never participated with the worship team, came forward to help. They both played musical instruments—but had been silently unwilling to work with the previous leader. Leadership abilities on the team, never before revealed, emerged as team members worked with new freedom and energy. Dismissing the dysfunctional leader didn't harm the church's worship; it enhanced it as the team stepped up its performance. The worship team members knew a change was needed. They were relieved and supportive, not angered, when the church's leadership made the decision to dismiss him. Sometimes our followers wonder what takes us so long to discover what they have known all along—a person is inadequate and needs to be replaced.

When you are reluctant to confront a problem employee or volunteer, it demoralizes other followers who work with or for that person. You might think being patient with a problem employee would be admired or appreciated by other employees. And to an extent it is. This is particularly true when poor performance results from a temporary problem (health crisis, family tragedy, etc.). Almost everyone wants coworkers to be treated fairly. Most people want others to have every opportunity to succeed. But most people also understand that being treated fairly means having clear performance expectations and being held accountable to meet those standards. When a volunteer or employee is doing a good job, and someone else around him or above him isn't, corrective action is expected. When you don't respond, capable employees or volunteers may become discouraged. They wonder why they should continue to do their jobs well. They wonder if you are out of touch with your organization. They wonder if you are a weak leader who can't make tough decisions. All these doubts reflect poorly on your leadership, undermine your effectiveness, and limit the progress of your church or organization. Being fair with team members, with *all* team members, includes holding them accountable to agreed-upon performance standards and replacing those who don't measure up. Those who are doing a good job will respect you when you make these decisions.

While these are all generally positive outcomes, sometimes a termination (no matter how justified) will be ugly. Terminated employees may lash out in anger, threaten or start legal action against you, or spread misinformation about their termination throughout the organization or through the media. Dismissed volunteers may resent your decision and leave your church or organization. Other team members may not understand the reasons for your decision (and often can't be told because of confidentiality requirements), may question the fairness or the appropriateness of your action (based on the information they have or their assumptions about the situation), or may be demoralized by your decision (feeling it could happen to them or friends they work with). Even though these things might happen, you must still make the best decision for the long-term health of your church or organization. If you have made the right decision, the passage of time will prove the wisdom of your action. Don't let the fear of a negative reaction keep you from making a tough but necessary decision. Weather the storm and trust God to make things right in time.

Deciding to Terminate Someone

While no checklist guarantees a right decision in every instance on such a delicate and complicated matter as dismissing someone, there are key points to consider in making and carrying out your decision. Here is a summary of some issues to consider as you work through the termination process.

Be fair.

When you are thinking about terminating an employee or volunteer, be sure you evaluate the person objectively. Have you defined your expectations? Have you coached the person to meet those expectations? Have you measured the results (or lack of them) and discussed those measurements with the person? Have you given the person appropriate support, tools, and training to make the changes you have mandated? Have you allowed enough time for the person to make the changes required? Are you keeping the focus on the person's performance, not on personality? In other words, are you terminating the person because of poor performance or because you just don't like him or don't want to work with him? These are all important issues to consider. Terminating, dismissing, or reassigning a person has profound implications for individuals and for your organization. Be as objective as possible in your analysis. Base your decisions on measured, documented behavior instead of your hunches or impressions. Be as fair as possible in your deliberations.

Be ethical.

Certain situations make removing a person the wrong decision even though his performance would justify his dismissal. For example, if a long-term employee is nearing retirement, it isn't right to dismiss him without regard for his longevity and soon-to-be received retirement benefits. Doing this, even when the person's performance is limiting your team, will significantly damage morale and diminish the respect your followers have for you. One leader arrived at his new post and discovered a twenty-year employee he deemed ineffective. The leader dismissed him a few months before he was eligible to retire. While his coworkers recognized some performance deficiencies, they were incensed that he was terminated. Board members were equally disappointed in the decision. The decision and its aftermath proved to be this leader's undoing. He couldn't overcome the loss of trust his decision caused throughout the organization.

Employees who are sick or temporarily unable to perform at their best also deserve special treatment. What you may compromise in organizational performance will be offset by the morale-building decision of supporting a hurting person through a difficult time. Even though replacing a person will improve organizational performance in the short run, it may not be the best decision for the long haul. Do the right thing to care for persons and treat them ethically. Be sensitive to human vulnerability and give greater latitude in special circumstances. Your ministry will thrive, in the long run, because of these compassionate, patient choices.

Be generous.

Part of treating people fairly and ethically includes being generous with them as they leave your organization. When a long-term volunteer or employee is performing poorly, it's easy to focus on recent events and overlook her total contribution to the organization over a longer time frame. It's important to celebrate a person's total contribution with appropriate recognition even though recent performance mandates a change. Recognition might include a verbal affirmation, written commendation, celebration appropriate to their length of service, and gifts or commemorative items. Just because a person is being removed from her position doesn't mean she hasn't made a contribution in the past that deserves to be recognized and celebrated. Being generous with praise, recognition, or appropriate closure activities can make a termination more palatable—both for the displaced person and other team members.

Being generous, in some situations, may include financial considerations. When an employee nearing retirement needs to be replaced, it should be done without financial harm to the employee. When an employee is terminated, a severance payment to assist with his transition, future job training, or personal expense might be appropriate. When a volunteer is removed, offering to find him another ministry position or help train him for another role in your church or ministry may also be appropriate. Not all terminations are adversarial. Some people deserve help in moving to their next assignment, particularly if their termination results more from changes in the organization than deficiency in their performance. If the expectations of the organization about their positions have changed (through no fault of their own), assisting with their transition (like with placement costs) may be the right thing to do. While this must be done carefully to avoid setting precedent or communicating favoritism, it can be a generous part of helping terminated employees move toward a more positive future.

Another example of generosity is allowing a person to resign from his position, rather than be terminated. On some occasions, when explaining to people why they are about to be terminated, employees will ask if they can resign instead. For some people, being terminated is an embarrassment to avoid. There is usually no compelling reason to deny a person the opportunity to resign rather than be terminated, particularly if it enables him to preserve dignity, to save face as he explains his situation to others.

Be legal.

Many legal issues related to employment law come into play when you are terminating someone. If you lead a large organization, consult your human resources specialist who can help you comply with organizational policies and state and federal laws. In smaller organizations and most churches, this resource isn't available. In those cases, consult an attorney or other employment specialist to mitigate potential legal problems. A few dollars spent on the front end of this process may save thousands in the long run, not to mention preventing other negative fallout resulting from a mismanaged termination. Consulting an attorney and terminating a person within both the law and your organization's guidelines will *not* prohibit legal action from being taken against you. But doing so will make it far less likely those actions will have merit.

Be decisive.

When you have carefully worked through the process and are sure a person needs to be terminated, be decisive. Be sure of your decision and then take definitive action. An executive of a large international ministry said, "The worst mistake of my early career was waiting too long to make personnel decisions. I would know what needed to be done, but I just kept waiting for change that never happened. All waiting did was demoralize other followers and make me look weak and ineffective. I learned this valuable lesson: When a person has to go, sooner is better than later." When did he learn that lesson? When he was a young pastor of a small church, working with volunteers and part-time employees. So whether you are a small-church pastor leading volunteers or an executive overseeing hundreds of employees, the principle is the same. When you are sure a person has to be dismissed or reassigned, take action. Delay isn't in the best interest of the person in question or your organization.

Conclusion

Terminating an employee or removing a volunteer from your ministry team can be difficult. But a huge part of your leadership responsibility is managing people. You can't duck it or pass it off to someone else. Denial isn't an option. Delay won't solve the problem. Without courageous personnel decisions, your church or organization will suffer, underperforming personnel will flounder, other employees or volunteers will be discouraged, and your mission will be compromised. Decisions to limit or prevent these scenarios come with the territory when you assume a leadership role. The greater your influence, the larger your organization, the more likely you will make these kind of personnel decisions. Ask God for wisdom as you make these decisions, for humility as you implement them, and for courage as you manage the consequences—both for the good of God's *mission* and his *people*.

11

Taking a Courageous Stand

Courage has many faces—some sculpted in bold relief; others more subtle, yet equally profound. A person who gives his life in a moment of selfless sacrifice is an obvious, dramatic example of courage. My friend Adam died defending freedom and protecting innocent civilians from terrorist attacks. As a soldier, he chose to go into harm's way on behalf of others. He exemplifies courageous sacrifice. There are, however, other less dramatic ways courage is demonstrated in various life situations.

Sheri is also courageous. She gave birth to a handicapped child and was told to institutionalize him since he would live only a short time. She and her husband, Larry, made a different decision. They took Ethan home and made the sacrifices necessary for his care. He lived more than twenty years, never growing larger than a small child or developing beyond the capabilities of a toddler. This couple made a courageous choice based on their conviction about life, *all* life, being valuable to God.

A youth pastor noticed a man in his twenties trolling the youth group for dates. Since he was the son of prominent church members, most people considered his advances harmless flirting. But the youth pastor grew concerned as one girl became infatuated. He stepped in and limited the man's involvement as a youth worker. He wasn't surprised when the man's family became angry. He was shocked, however, when the girl's father also criticized him. His action to protect a naive girl became divisive among his followers.

An accountant in a Christian organization raised questions about internal financial operations of the ministry. His supervisors glossed over his complaints and refused to forward them to their governing board. He made a courageous decision to submit the information directly to the board. His supervisors were livid. They convinced the board that the complaints were bogus and pressured him to leave the organization. He did and was spared prosecution a few years later when state regulators shut the ministry down and prosecuted its senior leaders.

Eric is a missionary in the *favelas* (slums) of Rio de Janeiro, Brazil. He leaves his family each night and leads his team to work among the paramilitary thugs, drug dealers, and prostitutes who control the streets. He has been robbed, shot at, and had his life threatened on several occasions. Yet he keeps at it. When asked why, he replied, "The gospel's gotta get to 'em!" His passion drives him to courageously take the gospel into dangerous places among desperate people.

Courage has many faces. It's seen in a young soldier, a couple raising a handicapped child, a pastor who takes a moral stand, a businessman who insists on integrity, or a missionary in a dangerous place. Courage is sometimes demonstrated in a moment of glory and other times in quiet choices with long-lasting consequences. Taking a courageous stand means you do the right thing even when it's difficult or painful. Courage is shown by making tough choices based on personal convictions grounded in biblical standards.

In my book *The Character of Leadership*, courage as a character quality for leaders is considered from a variety of perspectives. My insights about courage included a study of more than six hundred references to fear (and related topics) in the Bible. Biblical leaders struggled with fear. Those struggles reveal fear is an old problem, a pervasive problem, and common problem for leaders. So if you feel fearful, that's nothing new. Courageous leadership isn't the absence of fear. It's acting in the midst of fear, not waiting until it abates. Courage is moving ahead while you are still afraid, not waiting until fear dissipates.

Making courageous leadership decisions requires discernment and skill. You can increase your capacity for making these decisions by implementing the following strategies. A courageous decision is usually a process, not an instantaneous or on-the-spot choice. Thinking the process through will help you make courageous decisions and manage the painful consequences you may experience. The following steps create a rubric to guide you along the way.

Choose a Worthy Issue

When deciding to take a courageous stand, make sure the issue really is worth the pain and potential sacrifice that may result. As a younger pastor, I was equally passionate about almost everything! One particular issue (don't even remember what it was) was consuming me, when a supportive church member stopped by to see me. In his late thirties, he was a prosecuting attorney and would soon become a judge. He had played fullback in college—a hard-charging, straight-shooting, no-holds-barred kind of guy. As we discussed the crisis du jour (again, no memory of what it was), he asked, "Is this really a hill you want to die on?"

What? How could he be going soft? Isn't every hill the same? If something matters, don't you fight to the death to establish your position? Isn't compromise a sign of weakness, of failed moral authority, or the absence of integrity? My hard-nosed, football-playing, criminal-convicting friend shocked me. He challenged me to differentiate issues into categories of relative importance. And coming from this particular friend, it was a startling insight. Some issues deserve a courageous battle, and frankly others don't. Choosing my battles was a new concept.

Developing discernment, the ability to appraise issues and situations appropriately, is a challenge for all leaders. Seeing things from God's perspective, practicing spiritual discernment, is the unique challenge and obligation for Christian leaders. Some issues matter more to God than others. We must adjust to his priorities. We must learn the difference between a preference, perspective, proverb, principle, conviction, and law. Only convictions and laws deserve a courageous stand. The other categories are escalating levels of belief, but they don't rise to the level of a conviction or law demanding courageous action.

A conviction is a personal standard based on the collective

wisdom of biblical instruction related to a specific subject. Convictions must be established when there is no "chapter and verse" detailing a subject in the Bible—for example, an issue like stem cell research. The collective wisdom of carefully considered theological conclusions based on biblical insights should form our convictions when a specific subject isn't addressed in the Bible. A law, on the other hand, is an absolute instruction from God that can't be compromised. For example, the biblical standard of sexual fidelity in marriage is clearly articulated in the Bible—no adultery!

Courageous leaders save their energy to stand up for convictions and laws. We don't squander it on lesser battles. While we may have preferences, perspectives, proverbs, or principles that guide our thinking, we won't die on the hill of projecting any of these on the people we lead. We make sure we choose our battles carefully, because once we take a courageous stand, we can't retreat. A courageous stand often has serious consequences.

Is there a litmus test to determine the relative importance of an issue? No. There's no foolproof formula. But there is an imaginary scenario, the "gun to the temple test" that helps. It works like this. If someone was holding a gun to your head and said, "Will you die for (fill in the blank with any issue)?" and your answer is yes, the issue is a conviction or a law. Don't treat this too flippantly. John, a pastor who served in Communist Romania, was interrogated this way on several occasions. Some leaders really have made these choices, rather than simply imagining them. But for the sake of illustration, imagine these scenarios.

If a gunman asked, "Will you deny Jesus Christ is the Son of God?" I would say no and take the consequences. If the gunman said, "Will you die defending the worship style you prefer in church?" I would say, "No, let's negotiate!" If the gunman asked, "Will you deny the Bible is God's Word?" again my answer would be no. If the gunman asked, "Will you die for a particular form of church government?" My answer would be, "No, and we don't even need to vote on it!" Most leaders have preferences about worship styles and church governance, but they aren't worth dying for.

It's often difficult for leaders to know how much energy to devote to upholding a position on some social or political issues. For example, opposing abortion falls into the category of a conviction requiring a courageous stand. Global warming, not as much. While both issues have moral dimensions, one clearly has greater ramifications—taking innocent life. Caring for the environment is a moral issue, but it doesn't rise to the same level as defending the unborn. On issues related to life, a courageous stand is required. On issues related to the environment, strong opinions and preferences may lead to worthy actions—but not to the point of the suffering inherent in taking a courageous stand.

As you mature as a leader, your list of courageous-stand issues will likely shrink. Some absolutes at age twenty-five just aren't as important at fifty. You will probably also deepen your core convictions about some remaining issues and be unwilling to compromise them. Still another change is that some issues not even on your mental radar twenty years ago are now quite significant. One example is the definition of marriage. How many Christian leaders saw this as a pressing issue twenty years ago? Now it's a defining social issue of our time. Upholding marriage as one man married to one woman for life is a conviction that can't be compromised. The stakes—spiritually, emotionally, socially, and culturally—are too high. Leaders who take a stand on this issue will pay a high price in the coming years.

When you are considering taking a courageous stand on any issue, ask yourself if it's really important enough to break relationships, expend financial resources, damage your reputation, or even risk your health or life. If not, perhaps negotiating a solution through compromise and accommodation is a more effective path. To be sure, some issues, decisions, problems, and situations require a courageous stand. Some things are worth fighting for! But be sure you make a wise evaluation before you make such a momentous decision. When a courageous stand is painful, knowing it's for a worthy cause will help sustain you through the turmoil.

Make a Measured Decision

Making a decision to take a courageous stand requires more than a snap judgment. In biblical terms, you need to count the cost (Luke 14:28). Practically speaking, how do you do that? Creating a "decision tree" or an interconnected set of procedures to work through a major decision can help. While these procedures are listed as steps, they are really a process. You initiate these steps in the order listed, but once you start a step, it will overlap with succeeding steps. For example, the first step is to pray. But don't pray once and then move on to the other steps. Pray first and then keep on praying as you implement the rest of the steps that follow.

Pray about it.

The foundation for effective decision making is prayer. Two kinds of prayer are important to making good decisions. First, pray devotionally each day for God to prepare you for whatever decisions you may face. Leaders don't always know what will surface each day, but praying devotionally to reconnect with God, submit to Jesus as Lord, and ask for the filling of the Holy Spirit is foundational. When you do this, you are more in tune with God's direction, no matter what comes your way throughout the day.

Second, pray about the specific issue you are trying to resolve. Ask God to direct you, empower you, give you wisdom, and enable you to see your problem from his perspective. Ask God for courage to make decisions and for grace to handle the consequences. If you are making a moral choice to stand for God's standards, ask him to take up your cause and protect you. When the early church faced persecution, Christians prayed, "And now, Lord, consider their threats, and grant that Your slaves may speak Your message with complete boldness" (Acts 4:29). The first step, and a continuing part of the decision-making process, is to pray. Pray daily. Pray devotionally. Pray specifically.

Gather information.

Before making a major decision, gather as much pertinent information as practically possible. This includes facts about the problem, related biblical principles, theological perspectives, and best practices others have used when facing the same problem. Gathering information also includes considering the possible consequences—intended and unintended—

of various solution scenarios. Again, in biblical terms, count the cost before you attempt a major project.

One caution—you will never have all the information about any problem, nor will you be able to identify all the possible consequences of all possible scenarios before you make a decision. Before staking his career (and later an entire company) on his decisions to build the Mustang and the minivan, legendary auto executive Lee Iacocca gathered significant information. The courageous aspect in these decisions was his willingness to build these paradigm-shifting vehicles when he had *enough* information, not all the information possible.

Iacocca once told an associate, "The trouble with you . . . is you went to Harvard, where they taught you not to take any action until you have got *all* the facts. You've got ninety-five percent of them, but it's going to take you another six months to get that last five percent. And by the time you do, your facts will be out of date because the market has moved on you. That's what life is all about—timing."[3]

While life is not *all* about timing, effective leadership is *largely* about timing. Effective leaders know it's impossible to have complete information in hand before making decisions. If you are planning to relocate your ministry, build new facilities, add new positions to your staff or volunteer team, lay out a new vision for your church, or adjust your doctrinal statement—gather as much information as possible. But you can't guarantee success through study. No perfect solution will be discovered if you just give yourself more time to gather more information. Good leaders develop a sense of having enough information to make a solid decision, while at the same time knowing risk is always involved in courageous leadership decisions. Some leaders have "analysis paralysis"—a wrongheaded belief their job is to analyze problems until the perfect solution emerges. When a leader has this malady, an organization suffers from his inability to make timely decisions.

Christian leaders should be examples of competent decision making based on incomplete information. Our ministries are supposed to be marked by faith and a willingness to follow God into the unknown. Consider Abraham. He heard God's direction to change locations and "went out, not knowing where he was going" (Heb. 11:8). You must lead responsibly—gathering the information needed to make informed decisions. But you must also lead with faith—taking people forward even though you will not fully know where you are going or all the problems you will encounter along the way.

Consult the stakeholders.

Your followers have a significant stake in the outcome of your decisions. While you can't (and shouldn't) consult with everyone in your church or organization about every decision, you must identify the stakeholders who will be impacted by a major decision and include them in your decision-making process. If you are a pastor considering taking a moral stand on a community issue, discuss your position with your church's leaders—not necessarily to get their approval, but for their counsel and support. If your decision is controversial, and most morally courageous decisions are, it's likely they will feel some of the fallout from your actions. It's only right, then, to include them in your decision-making process—if for no other reason than to prepare them for the onslaught that may come.

Family members are also significant stakeholders in your decisions. When you take a courageous stand, they may experience social or financial loss. Again, consulting with them isn't necessarily about obtaining permission or approval but rather to prepare them for the consequences of your actions. Do you remember the story (in chapter 3) about the pastor who confronted white supremacists in his church? His son actually told me the story. The pastor talked about his decision with this family and prepared them for what might happen. When he was fired, his son was proud of his father's stance. While the family suffered a financial setback, it was also a positive experience—particularly for this son who developed a lifelong respect for his father and other courageous ministry leaders. Remember, consulting your stakeholders—your leadership team and your family—isn't about getting their permission or approval. It's about preparing them for the possible consequences of your courageous action.

Deliberate about your decision.

You will, of course, deliberate all along—as you pray, gather information, and talk with your stakeholders. But this step is your initial attempt to formulate your specific position or decision. If you are considering a moral stand on a controversial issue—you need to plan how to announce your position, how to sustain your involvement, and how to manage the consequences. If you are considering a major ministry decision—like relocating your church or reorganizing your staff—you also need to make extensive plans for what you intend to do, how much it will cost, how your followers will be impacted, the proper timing for the decision, and how to manage both the expected and unexpected consequences.

To bring focus and specificity to this part of the process, write your ideas. Having the thoughts flow down your arm, through your fingers onto a keyboard, appear on a computer screen, and then into print will sharpen your focus. Deliberating is about mulling over options, meditating on possibilities, and writing proposal after proposal until you finally produce a clear expression of your position or plan. At that point, when you can clearly articulate your ideas, you are ready to share them with others and receive important feedback. But be careful not to distribute these initial drafts too broadly or too quickly. Use them as drafts to facilitate dialogue with your leaders and key constituents. Publishing these ideas too broadly will make later adjustments much more difficult.

Consult counselors.

Counselors are different from stakeholders. Stakeholders are followers or family members with a vested interest in the outcome of your decision. Counselors, on the other hand, are people outside your organization or family who can speak objectively with you about the problem or issue you are facing. Every leader needs consultants to turn to for reflection on major issues. These men and women have no agenda but the truth and no loyalty except to your welfare.

After praying, gathering information, consulting stakeholders, and deliberating/writing one or more possible solutions, put the information before your counselors for their input. Good leaders continually cultivate relationships with other insightful, experienced, godly leaders. The type of problem or situation determines which counselors to consult. If you are preparing to take a stand on a moral issue with public policy ramifications, consult theologians, physicians, and attorneys. If you are deciding about personnel, consult people who are skilled in human resources and relationships. If you are considering significant organizational changes, counsel with corporate executives or leaders of large ministry organizations.

Laying written plans out for a counselor to evaluate can be unnerving. They aren't always impressed and their critiques can be threatening. It's easy to become defensive about your proposed position or decision. Sometimes your consultants will tell you to back off a position or change your plans. Being defensive isn't helpful. Remembering they have your best interest at heart will help you receive their correction. And sometimes, when they affirm your plans, it's also unsettling because it means you are closer to taking a courageous stand or making a courageous decision.

Privately decide.

The next step in making a major decision is to decide privately. Making a decision privately means you come to a settled conviction. You know your position on a decision for your ministry will require courage to implement. Whatever the situation, you make a firm and final decision—*privately*—that you are convinced it is God's decision, as best you can discern and determine.

Coming to a private decision leads to no-flinch public decisions. Until you are prepared to stand in any setting, look any audience in the eye, and talk without any hesitancy about your position or decision—without any doubt, without any duplicity, without flinching—the decision isn't final and isn't ready for public debut. Getting a rock-solid inner peace about major decisions before you engage your followers publicly is essential. If your followers sense any wavering, they will be reluctant to move ahead. Courageous decisions, leading to sacrificial actions by your followers, will only have their full allegiance if they sense a quiet, settled, firm commitment in you. When a matter is settled in your heart, then (and only then) are you prepared to move to the next phase of decision making.

Publicly decide.

The next-to-last step in making a major decision is to decide publicly. This isn't as simple as just announcing your decision and receiving resounding affirmation. It requires leading a church or organization through a collective process similar to the steps you worked through to reach your private decision. The process of publicly deciding must be managed successfully to reach a unifying, momentum-producing conclusion. Announcing your position on a moral issue, for example, must be done in a way that supports, encourages, and educates your followers. It's more than making a speech or preaching a sermon. It may involve sharing some of the information that informed your decision, testimonies from stakeholders, or revealing some of the deliberation process that produced your final decision. Taking a courageous stand can be a profound teaching moment to educate and inspire followers.

While leaders generally do a good job informing followers when they take a courageous stand on a position, leaders often do a poorer job of leading a public decision process when collective, courageous action is required. Many leaders work for months through the process outlined above before coming to a final decision. They are excited about their conclusions and share them enthusiastically—to a tepid or even antagonistic response. Leaders are shocked and disappointed. Why? Because they forgot how long they had spent processing the decision and didn't make a realistic plan for their followers to do the same.

One pastor worked for months on a new vision and long-range plan for his church. He was very excited about it and rolled it out like this. He preached a major message (without any prepublicity except the church newsletter mailed the previous week) about the vision and distributed copies of his plan after the Sunday morning service. He announced it would be adopted (not voted on, *adopted*) at a church meeting the following week. The response, in this case, was apathy, not opposition. The church dutifully adopted the plan but never took any action toward its implementation. The pastor was discouraged by the results but never realized his failure to lead an adequate public decision-making process undermined any hope of congregational ownership of his plan.

Another pastor took a different approach. For about six months, he met with key church leaders in a process of discovering a new vision for their church. They prayed together and worked on the process intensely. The pastor was the chief visionary, writing ideas and circulating them for discussion among his leaders. They worked together to collectively create a new vision to present to the church. He then preached for five consecutive Sundays on the importance of vision, the process of developing the new statement, biblical principles of congregational discernment in decision making, and the key points of the new vision. The church was then invited to pray and discuss the new vision in small-group settings for the following two months. Finally, the church voted on the vision in a special meeting called just for this purpose. The church adopted the new statement enthusiastically and has been, at this writing, working with remarkable unity to fulfill that vision for more than a decade.

Leading a public decision-making process requires time to work through the issues involved and secure real support from your followers. When you make a major decision privately, you must then lead your followers through an appropriate process to come to a shared conclusion. This process must be appropriate to both your ministry setting and the issue you are deciding. You must allow time proportional to the gravity of the issue being considered to reach a shared conclusion. Don't fear doing this will derail your position or plan. If God is leading you, and your followers, you will come to the same conclusion. If not, there's no hope for real progress anyway.

Manage the results.

The last step in making a courageous decision is managing the results. Making a decision and thinking, "Well, that's done," is immature and shortsighted. When an interdenominational group of pastors in a small town banded together to create common policies about performing marriages (requiring premarital counseling, for example) the backlash was swift and pointed. They were accused of legalism, of "playing God," and of trying to dictate community moral standards. They had to stand their ground, continually interpret their position, explain their policies, and manage the people who tried to play one of them against the other. Making the decision was easy; managing the consequences over the next few years was much tougher. When you take a courageous stand, there will be consequences that must be managed. That's an important and often overlooked part of a good decision-making process.

Take Responsibility for Your Decisions

When you take a courageous stand, you should expect painful consequences. Immature believers think God will bail them out of every problem. Mature leaders know better. We make courageous decisions because they are right, not because we are promised positive results. One powerful example of this principle is the story of the three young men who faced death in a fiery furnace (Dan. 3). King Nebuchadnezzar ordered everyone to bow down and worship a large statue he had erected in his honor, or face being burned alive. Shadrach, Meshach, and Abednego refused. They were tossed into the fiery furnace, blazing so hot it killed the men who threw them in. God protected these courageous men and brought them out alive. That's the good news, the happy ending.

But when they went into the furnace, they had no assurance they would come out. They didn't take their stand against idolatry because they knew they would be protected.

They took it because they knew it was right. Their statement to the king made this clear: "If the God we serve exists, then He can rescue us from the furnace of blazing fire, and He can rescue us from the power of you, the king. But *even if He does not rescue us,* we want you as king to know that we will not serve your gods or worship the gold statue you set up" (Dan. 3:17–18, emphasis added).

Sometimes, when we take a courageous stand, God delivers us. Other times, we suffer the consequences of our choices. God alone determines those outcomes. When Paul was jailed in Philippi, God sent an earthquake to release him (Acts 16:26). Later, however, Paul spent two years in jail, waiting resolution of his case (Acts 24:27). God isn't obligated to deliver you and doesn't always bail out courageous leaders. Sometimes God allows leaders to suffer—for years—to accomplish his purposes through us and in us on his timetable.

Courageous leaders take responsibility for their actions. They resist the temptation to blame God or others for negative consequences. They also refuse to adjust their theology (God must not be blessing this decision since it's so painful.) or change their mind (I must have missed God's will since it turned out this way.) when trouble comes. When you make a difficult decision, expect some negative consequences. Some people won't like your position, some will question your motives, and others will challenge your spirituality. You may lose some followers who don't agree with the direction you are leading or don't want to pay the price for being associated with you. Nevertheless, like Martin Luther, sometimes you just have to say, "Here I stand," and accept the consequences of your decision.

Conclusion

One aspect of courageous leadership is initiating change. Leaders see what doesn't exist and try to create it. We see what isn't and try to turn it into what is! This requires leading people into the unknown, a painful process for some followers *and leaders*. But we simply can't duck our responsibility to lead change. Even when we see the pain coming, we still must make the tough call to press ahead.

And pressing ahead can be painful. Leading change, and managing the personal dynamics of the process, is the next subject for our consideration. Most books on change focus on the pain followers experience through the change process. Let's keep our focus on the self-inflicted pain you will experience as a change initiator. You know it will hurt, but you can't leave well enough alone! You are a leader and leaders change things. Rather than focusing on how to lead change, let's focus on how to manage yourself while leading change.

Leading a
Significant Change

Creating bumper stickers must be a lucrative field—there are so many of them! A slogan that might be a huge seller is: "Change is good. You go first." Most people say they like change, are future oriented, and welcome innovative ideas. But their response to change often contradicts that claim. Almost all of us are open to change—as long as it's in areas *we* want changed. But when asked to change in an area we don't think needs it, we resist. As a baseball purist, for example, I am still upset that the American League adopted the designated hitter rule in 1973. Everyone knows National League baseball is *real* baseball. And, no, I don't plan to change my mind!

If experiencing change is hard, leading change is even harder. A primary responsibility of leaders, however, is leading change. A team of researchers studied leadership as described and defined in thousands of publications covering the entire twentieth century. Their purpose was to define leadership, in one sentence, based on this extensive database. Their conclusion: "Leadership is an influence relationship among leaders and followers who intend real changes that reflect their mutual purposes."[4] *Real change* is at the core of leadership. This is the key phrase that distinguishes leadership from management (a different but also valuable discipline). Managers *implement* processes to produce or improve products or services. Leaders *invent* the processes, products, and services. Christian leaders facilitate real change—substantive, innovative, paradigm-changing, new-way-of-thinking breakthroughs in the churches and organizations they lead.

An overview of some basic theological themes underscores why Christian leaders are change agents. While God is unchanging, the world he created is constantly changing (weather, seasons, ocean tides, wildlife). God has worked progressively from creation to the church to fulfill his eternal redemptive purposes. God expects Christians to change—ever heard of the doctrine of sanctification? The metaphors of the Christian life—like vine to branches, stones to buildings—imply progress and growth. God's world is ever changing, his people are ever growing; so churches and ministries giving form to his mission must be changing. These organizations require leaders skilled at sensing God's direction and helping people move into the future.

How does one effectively lead change without pain? It can't be done. A subtle message in some books on leading change is if you just use "the correct process," it will always go well. Not so! No matter how carefully you plan a change or how skillfully you implement it, there's no surefire way to avoid the painful side of leading change. Rather than drift toward strategies for leading organizational change (valuable but not the focus of this book), let's focus on issues leaders struggle with when leading change, common mistakes leaders make by producing frustration with change management, and some fundamental aspects of the leader's role in bringing about real change.

Scars of Change or Lessons Learned the Hard Way

My soul is scarred from wounds received—some self-inflicted—while trying to lead change in churches and ministry organizations. My understanding of leading change as a young leader can be summarized by three strategies: teach the Bible (shaded to support the change I wanted), lecture people (on how and when I wanted the change done), and steamroll the opposition (since resistance is evidence of rebellion or failure to submit to authority). Any questions why my early attempts at leading significant change weren't very successful?

God, using his people, has largely extinguished these strategies from my leadership practices repertoire. The growth process has been painful, made more so by having to admit character flaws and leadership deficiencies revealed by my actions. To minimize your pain in leading change, go to school on my experiences and spare yourself some heartache. Here are some key insights learned along the way—most learned the hard way.

Change tolerance is proportional to relational trust.

When you ask followers to change, you are asking them to trust your promise that the future is better than the present. You are asking them to trust you with their time, money, and talents for projected or hoped-for results. You may be asking for sacrifice resulting in lost dreams or changed plans for them or their families. One church was building a new campus. The cochairs of the capital campaign were a married couple who owned a small company. On the day they launched the campaign, they told the church, "When we got married, we didn't have the money for a honeymoon. We vowed to take a trip to Australia for our twenty-fifth wedding anniversary. For the past twenty-five years, every month, through thick and thin, we have put something in our 'honeymoon fund.' Next year is our twenty-fifth anniversary. We have saved enough for our dream trip. But we have decided to give all the money to the building program instead."

What prompted this couple to make that sacrifice? First, they love God and are committed to his mission through their church. But second, they also trusted their pastor. They believed he was leading the church to do the right project, at the right time, in the right way, and for the right reasons. They trusted their pastor because he had proven himself over the years with a series of wise decisions in leading the church through lesser changes. When it came time for a multi-million-dollar project requiring sacrificial giving by everyone, they were willing to set the pace.

One of the biggest mistakes leaders make is attempting too much change too soon in their relationship with their followers. One young pastor-to-be sought my counsel, "Let me share my vision for my new church with you. Then I want your advice on how to fulfill it." He rolled out a magnificent vision of dramatic change. When he finished, my reply surprised him: "Go there and marry and bury a few people first."

Eagerly, and innocently, he was about to commit a cardinal sin of leading change—attempting change disproportional to the established level of relational trust. People follow people more than ideas or proposals. Real change runs successfully on the track of relational trust. After this young pastor has sat up all night with the family of a dying church patriarch, made some midnight trips to the hospital, been present for a few births, counseled couples back from the brink of divorce, baptized children of parents anxious to "get it right" with their kids, sung campfire songs at youth camp, and been on at least one trip when the bus broke down—*then* he will be ready to ask the church to follow him through significant change.

Even proven leaders must confirm relational trust before initiating major change. Fortunately, after you have established a track record of trustworthy leadership, this becomes easier as you lead in new settings or in new projects. After many years of proven leadership, you will be extended "presumed trust"—meaning your new followers expect to trust you because of your past leadership record. But still, confirming their trust by your actions is essential for turning presumed trust into *actual* trust when leading in a new setting or in a new venture. Establishing relational trust in a ministry organization is somewhat different from establishing it as a church leader. Church leaders establish relational trust largely through providing ministry (as previously illustrated). Organizational leaders, while they care for their employees, aren't pastors. They earn trust by making consistent decisions, improving the work environment, and delivering on promises made to employees.

To avoid some of the painful side of leadership, build relational trust before you launch major change initiatives. It seems this may slow your change process. But building relational trust doesn't delay your process. It's the *first step in the process* of leading any significant change successfully. Without it, you may be doomed to disappointment from the beginning. So check the trust level to be sure it will support the change you are proposing. Failure to accurately appraise this leadership dynamic will be painful.

Change is more an emotional transition than a factual, logical, or rational decision.

When asked to change, people often become frustrated or angry. Emotions quickly boil to the top when something or someone dear is threatened. Most leaders tend to make decisions based on facts. We like data. We analyze a problem and imagine solutions leading to proposed changes. It seems like such a clean process, until a fact-based change proposal collides with feelings-based followers.

In my first pastorate, it seemed obvious our church needed to relocate. After a few years of steady growth, we had two full Sunday morning services and two Sunday schools using every classroom (and some converted trailer houses we stuck on the property). The facts—current attendance, growth potential, packed buildings, ugly trailers, terrible location, and absence of parking—mandated relocation. After processing this decision with church leaders for months, it was agreed that we would announce a feasibility study to consider the possibility of relocating. Note—not an announcement to relocate, just a feasibility study!

One member confronted me after the announcement and said, "All my daughters were married in this church. My children and grandchildren have all been baptized here. We've lived near this church for years. Why are you taking our church from us?" When I replied, "We aren't taking your church from you. We are trying to make room for more families in the future to have a similar experience as your family," he stormed off, angrily huffing and muttering.

Over the next few weeks, even when we were miraculously provided ten acres of property within one mile of our current location, angry conversations continued. Attempts to confront those emotional responses with the facts were unsuccessful. The only result was: I was also getting angry! In the midst of this turmoil, God helped me understand my members' anger was a symptom of grief. They were experiencing a profound sense of loss associated with leaving the old building. My tactics changed. Instead of presenting the facts, my role shifted to helping them process grief, much like working through the death of a loved one.

Experiencing change is emotional because, for many people, *change is a grieving process.* They are turning loose of something familiar and embracing the unknown. Their comfort zone has been shattered and new beginnings are required. When an organization restructures, for example, the following losses can occur. Employees lose relationships, titles, work space, and formal and informal networks through which they did their jobs. Even in situations where most embrace the positive possibilities of the new structure, there's still some grief involved in the change.

Helping people process change is more about helping them work through the stages of grief—anger, denial, bargaining, adjustment—than it is arguing facts with them. A few years ago a friend was speaking at a major conference. This was during the height of the conflicts over worship styles. For the first time, this particular conference was using a contemporary worship band. The afternoon session attracted an older, mostly senior adult crowd. As the band played, the tension in the room rose with each drumbeat.

When my friend stepped up to speak, he said, "I sense some of you don't like this music." There was nervous laughter and quiet murmuring of agreement. "But if your grandchildren would come to church with you every Sunday," he continued, "would you be willing for this to be your church's worship style?" A lot of tension left the room as heads all around nodded yes. Rather than argue the facts about the need for varieties of worship styles, he appealed to the hearts of those grandparents, many who had grandchildren who had left the church. Change management is about helping people at the heart level, not just the head level, to adjust to the future they are being asked to embrace.

You can avoid some leadership pain if you stop arguing and debating with people about accepting change. Instead, listen to the underlying reasons for their resistance and help them process those feelings. You may dismiss this as too touchy-feely, too much pandering to emotions. You may feel this is a waste of time and slows your trailblazing approach to change. But if you ignore the emotional realities of change leadership, you do so at your peril. Keep arguing the facts if you enjoy self-inflicted pain.

Change resistance is proportional to our hierarchy of core commitments.

Some changes are perceived as minor changes, others as major changes. Of course, change is like surgery: major if it's on me, minor if it's on you! Leaders usually determine the difference between major and minor changes by the financial cost or the time needed to implement the change. The real differentiation, however, is based on a person's perception of how the change will impact his core commitments. Notice the progression in the following chart.

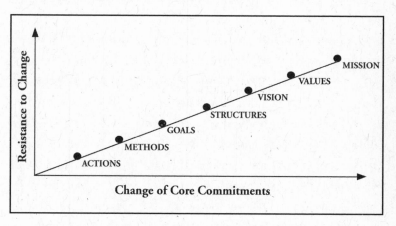

The chart ranks a range of commitments that matter to people. The easiest for your followers to change is their actions. The hardest is their mission (reason or purpose for existing). Resistance to change increases as a proposed change is perceived to impact evermore significant life commitments.

Consider this example. If you ask a Bible study leader to read a new curriculum piece and give you his opinion about it (action), you are unlikely to meet much resistance. If you ask him to change from a lecture method to teaching through group discussion (method), you may have some resistance unless you offer training and support. Asking the teacher to change from a discipleship-oriented curriculum to an outreach-oriented curriculum (goals of instruction) is likely to increase the resistance. If you move to the next step, asking him to change from teaching a class to organizing several classes (threatening his structures), he is likely to move from resistance to opposition. Suppose you then ask him to quit teaching (striking at vision, values, or even mission) and become a soloist. He is likely to leave altogether!

This doesn't mean you shouldn't initiate these changes. It means you must design strategies to educate this person about the need for the change and help him understand how the future you envision for him can be an expression of a new vision, values, and mission. A similar process happens corporately when churches or ministries attempt major changes. Changing actions usually meets little resistance. But as you change methods, goals, structures, vision, values, and mission, the resistance intensifies. Again, this doesn't mean you shouldn't initiate changes to the core commitments of your organization. It simply means the higher on the scale the change impacts your followers, the more deliberate and thorough your change implementation strategy must be. Failure to recognize this is a recipe for leadership pain.

Change, no matter how well received, won't be embraced by everyone.

Leaders crave unity. We want everyone to move forward with us. Part of leading change, however, is accepting the cold, hard fact that not everyone will embrace every change.

When we were considering the church relocation mentioned earlier, one couple's response left me puzzled. They

were among the hardest workers and most faithful supporters, sacrificial givers, and loyal members of our church.
When they first heard of the possibility of relocation, they
spoke against it. They offered bizarre reasons like, "The soil
on the site won't support any buildings." They predicted
the worst—"The church will change and people won't like
it." These were reasonable, usually supportive people. We
had many conversations about their concerns. They weren't
mean-spirited. They were just resolutely against relocation.

When the time came to vote on the project, the church
voted almost unanimously to move. But this couple voted
their conviction—*no*. They never changed their minds
although they seemed to enjoy the new facility after moving
with the church. This couple typifies one group of people—
laggards—and how they respond to change. Laggards are
against change and express their opposition either actively
(like the couple above) or passively (by remaining quiet but
not supporting the change).

Leaders often make the mistake of trying to convince
every laggard to enthusiastically support every change. This
is, generally, a waste of time. It's better to accept the fact that
a small percentage of people in any church or organization,
depending on the change at hand, will never support it. And,
if the issue were different, some laggards would become supporters and some supporters would then become laggards.
There are almost always laggards, only their names change
depending on the change proposed. The best strategy for
working with laggards, after you have clearly communicated
the change and effectively invited them to participate, is to
leave them alone. Usually they tag along quietly after the
change is successfully implemented.

Another group of change resisters are those who react so negatively they won't ever support the change. These people are *leavers*. Church members may leave and employees may quit rather than move into the future with you. Losing people is difficult. Most Christian leaders, especially pastors, have a shepherd's heart. We want our flock to stay together. Losing people is painful because we feel we have failed by not keeping everyone together.

We also ache when we lose people because we need every person to make major changes successfully. When you lose people from a church, you lose workers, donors, and people who might be essential for major change to be implemented well. When you lose employees or key volunteers from your organization, you lose skill, experience, knowledge, and networks. The changes you have initiated may be slowed or derailed by having to replace key personnel you were counting on to help you move the change forward. All these reasons make losing people during major change painful for leaders.

Leaders are sometimes reluctant to propose major change because they fear losing people. Get over that fear. Determine to do what is best for the whole organization, not what will keep the peace with detractors. Accept that any change has the potential of producing laggards and leavers. While you want your church or organizational family to stay together, unity at the expense of accomplishing God's mission isn't genuine unity.

Consider another perspective on leavers. Pastors and senior ministry leaders often move from one church or ministry to another and claim, "God is finished with me here." That's a valid claim. God uses leaders for a season. No pastor or other leader is permanent. Even if they are long-tenured, retirement or death eventually means a new leader will come. When a leader departs, having made the above claim, church members, board members, and employees generally celebrate the departure and pray God's blessing on the leader's future ministry.

Why is this principle only applicable to leaders? Why doesn't every church member or ministry employee have the same privilege of leaving, with everyone's blessing, when they feel they no longer fit and need to find a more appropriate ministry setting? When someone leaves a ministry organization, the frequent assumption is that something must be wrong. That isn't always the case. Because of a distorted view of unity, we expect once a person joins a church or a ministry, she will remain for her lifetime. That's an unrealistic expectation. When you propose a major change, some members or employees may not go with you into the future. They have gifts, skills, interests, and perhaps a sense of calling incompatible with the future you propose. When someone leaves your organization in these circumstances, his departure should be acknowledged positively and his past contribution celebrated. Nothing is necessarily wrong. Everyone is free to pursue his or her preferred future.

Sometimes when people leave, it's a blessing in disguise. It may be painful when it happens, but if they remain as disgruntled distracters (not laggards who are opposed but generally willing to go along), it undermines the change and possibly creates an even more painful conflict in the future. Unless you are forcing people to leave to further your personal agenda, some departures may be the best thing in the long run. In these cases, short-term pain produces long-term gain.

Change takes longer than you think it will.

Change, real change, takes time—often a long time. A major change involves significant preparation, implementation over time, and a prolonged effort to support the change until it becomes the new normal for your organization. One church decided to change from a Sunday school small-group structure to a home-based cell structure. The church took one year to study the options before making the decision. Then it took another year to train new leaders and create a new organization. The change was then implemented. For a full year the problems, challenges, and surprises had to be dealt with until the new approach was fully functional. Whether the change is a new organization, a new curriculum, a new facility, or a new church start, it will take time—perhaps years to really make it happen.

In light of this, there are two questions to answer before attempting major change. The first is: "Are you sure this is the right change?" As a leader, be sure you are initiating the right change because it will consume you for months or years. And beyond your investment, consider the investment of your followers. Before you ask them to commit to a major change, be sure you are convinced it's a divine directive.

The second question: "Are you committed to seeing the change through to full implementation?" Note the phrase "full implementation." That means you can leave only when the change has been accomplished to a point of stability in your organization, and your departure won't jeopardize the church or ministry. For example, it doesn't seem appropriate for a pastor to lead a major building program resulting in massive debt and then resign, leaving the church to pay it off.

The job isn't finished until the bills are paid. Other people shouldn't have to pay for changes we initiate.

When you are considering a major change, double the time you think it will take to do it. One veteran leader said, "Right, and then double it again!" Most leaders are far too optimistic about the pace of change. Having realistic expectations about the time involved will lower your frustration threshold and alleviate some of the pain associated with waiting for major change to be fully implemented.

Creating a Climate for Change

As already indicated, this chapter is about your response to the pressure and difficulty of leading change. It isn't primarily about developing change-management strategies. There is, however, one overarching strategic action foundational to successfully implementing any change process. As the leader, you are the only person in your organization who can do this. You have the unique platform through your position to create a climate for change. Doing the following can help create this climate, no matter the kind of step-by-step change-management process you later initiate.

Picture a preferred future for your organization.

My earliest attempts at creating a climate for change included browbeating my followers for their inadequacy, telling them how bad they were, and reminding them how good my experience had been in my previous ministry setting. For some mysterious reason, that didn't work!

It's incongruous to tell people how inadequate they are and then tell them they are adequate to fulfill your dream, if they will only get on board. We forget church members or ministry employees *are where they have been led*. If you are new in your setting, they followed your predecessor. If you have been in your position for a while, they followed you. Either way, a negative approach to their present circumstances is counterproductive. Telling the truth about your current situation, without blaming past leaders for their decisions or your followers for willingly supporting them, is a far better approach. Harping on how bad things are and how dumb your followers are for being in their present state is pointless.

To create a climate for change, focus your energy on creating a picture of a preferred future. Communicate your dream for what can be more than your criticism for what is. When you do this, followers will evaluate their present state without feeling threatened. In doing so, they are much more likely to cooperate on the change strategy you later ask them to implement.

Encourage dialogue about the future.

Too many leaders start a major change process by telling their followers what needs to happen rather than initiating dialogue about what might happen. Dialogue is threatening to some leaders. They fear losing control of the conversation and, therefore, the outcomes. But that isn't what usually happens. Remember this powerful fact about dialogue: The person asking the questions controls the conversation.

A wise leader asks the right questions to get people thinking about the future. Here are four of my favorite questions to facilitate this process:

1. If we fulfill the Great Commission in our community (or through our ministry organization), what would it look like?
2. If another fifty, one hundred, or one thousand (depending on your setting) people joined our church, what would have to change to meet their needs?
3. When we celebrate our (tenth, twentieth, or next significant) anniversary, what are the accomplishments you dream our organization will celebrate that day?
4. Suppose our church (or organization) didn't exist. You were given the money and power to start it over. What would it be like?

Ask these questions in formal and informal settings to promote dialogue about the future in churches and ministry organizations. Formal settings include retreats, committee meetings, or staff meetings—including occasional sessions devoted specifically to vision development or a change-initiating process. Informal settings include lunch with key leaders, over coffee when members or employees gather informally, or while riding in the car to ministry functions. One rural pastor who led his church through remarkable change told me, "I drink coffee most mornings at the cotton gin and have lunch a few times a week at the diner. That's where we make most of our church decisions. We may vote on them at church, but we talk through them someplace else." Brilliant leadership by a pastor who understands how to guide dialogue related to managing change.

Don't misunderstand the concept of dialogue. It isn't manipulating people into agreeing with you. It doesn't mean everyone must be consulted on every matter or every idea has to be included in the final decision. Dialogue with key leaders, employees, or stakeholders engages people in the process and creates a climate for working toward real change. Dialogue is valuable because your questions give people a preview of your thinking and where you and they might be going. Dialogue can also help you see shortcomings in your ideas or time frame for change. But perhaps it's most valuable because it helps people feel connected to the process, to feel like insiders on leadership decisions. Once, when working on a major visioning process, we invited every employee—every secretary, custodian, landscaper, manager, director, and vice president—to participate through focus group dialogue and providing written input. When the process concluded, several employees thanked me, and one said, "No matter if you use my ideas or not, it's great to be part of such an important process." That's the power of dialogue. Eventually you will articulate the major changes you believe must happen. But do that later in the process, after appropriate dialogue, not at the beginning before people are ready for it.

Develop major change proposals in a group context.

Some leaders have the "Moses on the mountain" mentality about receiving God's direction for their ministry. While that model worked once for Moses, major ministry decisions today are usually best made in the context of a small group. Every leader needs a small group of trusted colleagues who partner to develop major change initiatives. These groups function best when they are not concerned with day-to-day programs and operations and are primarily devoted to thinking, praying, and developing strategies for the future. For a pastor, this is usually a group of elders or deacons or some other form of governing group. In a ministry organization, board members, senior leaders, or department directors often form this kind of group. Again, while some time must be spent on operational problems, they should also have primary responsibility for thinking about the future and major changes required to move the organization forward.

Whether you are considering a new facility, a radical reorganization, a major staff addition or change, or another paradigm-shifting decision about your organization—you will almost always make a better decision, more readily embraced by your followers, if you make it with a group that represents them and has their confidence. We romanticize solo leaders who ride tall in the saddle. Those people are also the easiest to shoot! Most of the time, we are more effective if we ride with a posse.

Conclusion

Leading change can be a lonely, painful process. But by understanding some of the dynamics about change and how to create a climate for change, you can reduce your frustration. There are many good resources for developing step-by-step management of the change process. Learn all you can about long-range planning, strategic planning, and the visioning process. Learn the skills necessary to effectively implement whatever processes you choose. But no matter how capable you become, you will still be susceptible to the painful side of change leadership because of the unpredictability of leading people. Leading change is painful, but the rewards of following God by faith into his future outweigh the pain. So keep leading change—one adventurous aspect of ministry leadership.

Part of leading change is modeling the future you are challenging your followers to embrace. The sacrifices involved in becoming a role model for change can be painful. We turn our attention now to counting and paying the cost of being a pacesetting example inspiring others to move forward by faith.

Modeling a Challenging Commitment

One of the unique aspects of Christian leaders is the expectation that we will be role models. Leading by personal example is an integral part of Christian leadership. Before we can lead others to make significant commitments, we must model those commitments. This can be painful when we must sacrifice to set the pace by our example. When leading a fund-raising campaign, for instance, one leader gave 5 percent of his salary to his organization for the duration of the campaign. That gift modeled the sacrifice and commitment he wanted other donors to make. Making that gift was a personal challenge, but also a required sacrifice to establish credibility before asking others to join him in giving. Being a model of what we want followers to be or do can be costly— and painful in other ways as well.

A pastor wanted his church to increase its prayer focus. He started a daily early morning prayer meeting to facilitate that goal. Adjusting his schedule required personal discipline and forsaking late-night leisure activities. Another leader wanted to increase Scripture memory throughout his ministry. He founded a group that met monthly for support and accountability as followers memorized Scripture passages. Setting the pace in this effort required new discipline and honesty to admit when he hadn't kept up his memory work. Another leader wanted to promote humility among his men's group. So taking a twenty-first-century tack on foot washing, he shined everyone's shoes during their next meeting. It was humbling, yet effective, as men reflected on the powerful example of service shown by a surgeon shining their shoes. Setting the pace as a leader can be painful, but it comes with the territory of Christian leadership.

Establishing yourself as a role model for others may seem awkward or presumptuous. It can be, depending on your attitude, but modeling shouldn't be avoided as an essential leadership strategy because it might be abused or misused. Modeling, as we will see later, is a biblical expectation and strategy for Christian leaders. It's not only a strategy used by biblical leaders, but also one that they advocated their followers implement to transmit skills and information necessary to expand God's kingdom. Modeling says, "Observe my life, follow my example, do what I do." Modeling requires a person step forward, often boldly, to set the pace for others to follow. Charles Barkley, former NBA all-star player infamously said, "I am not a role model." As a Christian leader, making that claim isn't an option.

Reluctant Role Models

Some potential leaders, particularly younger leaders, are reluctant to assume the mantle of Christian leadership and serve as role models. They are willing to work on a team or be part of a project. They value collaboration and shared effort. They are content to be part of a group but don't want to put themselves in the leadership spotlight. They want to blend in, not stand out. They struggle with being "the leader," with assuming the authority and responsibility that comes with being in charge. Some go further and lament hierarchical organizational structures as out-of-date relics of a command and control philosophy from the past. You may have this perspective. If so, what causes this reticence, this aversion to being identified as a leader, to putting yourself forward as a model of Christian commitment and service?

Some potential leaders are put off by arrogant leaders whose style includes self-promotion and abuse of power. They wrongly assume that being a prominent leader means a person must be autocratic or dictatorial. While some leaders do abuse authority, most don't. Rejecting becoming a leader because of the sins of a few is unwise. Just because some leaders are arrogant, abusive, or autocratic doesn't invalidate the need for assertive leadership and the importance of a person emerging as the leader of a church or organization.

Another reason some are reluctant to lead is a false understanding of humility. To be a leader isn't antithetical to Christian humility. Humility isn't self-abasement. Humility is appropriate self-appraisal, seeing yourself as God sees you. It's adopting God's perspective on who you are and what you are assigned to do. Being humble means you accept

God's assignment and submit yourself for his service. If God has made you a leader, obedience requires you to accept the assignment. Doing God's will, God's way, leads to humility, not arrogance. This is true even if God calls you to a prominent leadership role.

A third reason some people resist becoming a leader is the abuse they observe veteran leaders enduring. One young man said, "I will never become a pastor because of how a church treated my dad." While he had obvious leadership gifts and many people saw evidence of God's call in his life, he refused to accept any ministry leadership role for several years. Finally he realized the abuse his father had endured was an excuse for his dereliction of duty, not a valid reason to reject leadership responsibilities. By the way—his father never abandoned his leadership calling, despite the abuse he endured from not one but two churches that mistreated him and his family. Real leaders know the road is difficult but don't give up their responsibility just because it's hard. Be careful not to take up offense on behalf of abused leaders and disobey God by using it as an excuse for your disobedience. That, too, will be a painful side of leadership—but in ways you may not have anticipated as God disciplines you.

Some refuse to lead because of a genuine sense of inadequacy. You may wonder, considering your weaknesses and foibles, how God could use someone like you in leadership. Feeling inadequate to lead can be healthy if it deepens your dependence on God. These feelings are only unhealthy when you use them as an excuse for not leading. When Jesus called Peter to leave fishing and assume a kingdom leadership role, Peter confessed, "Go away from me, because I'm a sinful man, Lord!" (Luke 5:8). For Peter, a Jewish man, to call himself a sinner was a startling admission. The word *sinner* means "filthy, rotten, or dirty." He was expressing his opinion of himself in contrast to Jesus. How would you have responded if you were Jesus?

Jesus responded, "Don't be afraid. . . . From now on you will be catching people!" (v. 10). Jesus had insight into Peter's character. He understood how volatile the next few years would be as Peter learned to follow him fully. Jesus also knew Peter would sleep through his garden temptation and betray him just prior to the Crucifixion. But Jesus was willing to use an inadequate follower, to turn him into a leader, even though he had serious deficiencies. Peter was the leader among the Twelve and became the leader of the early church after Jesus' ascension. But even after being with Jesus for many years, experiencing the Holy Spirit's power in remarkable ways, and rising to prominence in the early church (Acts 2–4; 10; 15), Peter was still not a perfect leader. At the peak of his influence, after leading for years, Paul confronted Peter about a major breach of Christian doctrine and practice (Gal. 2:11–14). Clearly Jesus calls and uses inadequate leaders in his work. You can't plead inadequacy as a disqualifier from Christian leadership. If that were a legitimate excuse, there wouldn't be any leaders!

Another reason some people won't assume a leadership role is an aversion to public scrutiny. Leaders live public lives. Their decisions are dissected, analyzed, and sometimes ridiculed. That's painful! Some reject becoming a leader because they simply don't want the pressure of life on stage. They would prefer to work behind the scenes, without the pressure of being observed and emulated, discussed and critiqued. Review chapter 6 if you need a refresher on how to live in the spotlight of leadership expectations.

If you have read this far, you have probably settled the issue of becoming a leader. If that's a settled issue, then being a role model—an example of Christian service and growth—also needs to become a settled conviction. Modeling, particularly modeling challenging commitments, is part of your job description. More than a leadership strategy, it's a biblical expectation. Let's discover why by considering how biblical leaders understood and applied this concept.

Modeling Is Biblical

Christian leaders must use biblical strategies to do their work well. Before setting yourself up as a role model, it's appropriate to ask if doing so is an acceptable biblical strategy. The answer is clearly yes. On several occasions both Paul and Peter wrote other leaders with specific instructions to be examples to their followers. Paul often challenged his converts to imitate him in order to become more fully devoted followers of Jesus (those terms are in italics in the following Scriptures).

Paul wrote his protégé Timothy, "No one should despise your youth; instead, you should *be an example* to the believers in speech, in conduct, in love, in faith, in purity" (1 Tim. 4:12). Two key thoughts emerge from this short exhortation. First, Timothy was challenged to be an example for his followers. And second, Timothy was a young man but still had the responsibility of being a role model because he was a pastoral leader. You may think you are excused from being an example, a role model, because of your youth or inexperience. Not so. If you are in a leadership role, even if you are younger or less experienced than others, you are still responsible to set an example worthy of being followed.

Paul wrote another of his trainees, Titus, "Set *an example* of good works yourself, with integrity and dignity in your teaching" (Titus 2:7). Titus was challenged to be a role model of good works and sound teaching. Like Timothy, he was a first-generation Christian leader who may have felt overwhelmed by the responsibility thrust upon him. Nevertheless, Paul clearly challenged Titus to be a good example, to be a role model.

Peter wrote about the same idea in his instruction to the elders who received his first letter: "I exhort the elders among you: shepherd God's flock among you, . . . not lording it over those entrusted to you, but *being examples* to the flock" (1 Pet. 5:1–3). Peter expected elders to be role models, actively demonstrating the character and actions they desired in their followers. Christian leaders aren't armchair quarterbacks, barking signals and expecting others to run the plays. We are on the field, in the game, guiding the action— a player/coach setting the pace. The most effective leaders of the early church, Paul and Peter, expected this of themselves and those they trained. We should do no less.

Paul instructed his disciples to be examples, to emulate his common practice of challenging believers to imitate him. Paul wrote the Corinthians a summary about his perspective on being a role model, "Be *imitators of me*, as I also am of Christ" (1 Cor. 11:1). Earlier in the same letter, Paul wrote, "I'm not writing this to shame you, but to warn you as my dear children. For you can have ten thousand instructors in Christ, but you can't have many fathers. Now I have fathered you in Christ Jesus through the gospel. Therefore I urge you, be *imitators of me*" (1 Cor. 4:14–16).

As a leader, Paul was comfortable telling other believers to follow his example. By doing so, they would become more fully devoted followers of Jesus. He used the illustration of a father's influence—subtle, powerful, and permanent—to communicate how influential leaders are as role models. Children are profoundly influenced by their father's example. That influence can be either positive or negative, but all children bear their father's mark. Christian leaders, like fathers, have the opportunity to profoundly influence their followers by their example. Most of what children learn from their fathers is by intuition and observation. It's much the same with your followers who are changed more by copying your actions than by hearing your instructions.

Paul combined both themes—being a role model and expecting his trainees to be role models—as he continued, "This is why I have sent to you Timothy, who is my beloved and faithful child in the Lord. He will remind you about my ways in Christ Jesus" (1 Cor. 4:17). Paul not only expected to be a role model, but he sent Timothy with instructions to use his life as an example of commitment to Jesus. As a Christian leader, you are a role model. You are responsible to model challenging commitments. And your followers should know you well enough to use your life as an example for others when teaching and illustrating principles of Christian living.

Paul wrote two other churches with instructions about imitating him. He told the Philippians, "Join in *imitating me*" (Phil. 3:17), and affirmed the Thessalonians because they "became *imitators of us* and of the Lord" (1 Thess. 1:6).

He later amplified the same theme in a second letter to the Thessalonians, "Now we command you, brothers, in the name of our Lord Jesus Christ, to keep away from every brother who walks irresponsibly and not according to the tradition received from us. For you yourselves know how you must *imitate us*: we were not irresponsible among you; we did not eat anyone's bread free of charge; instead, we labored and toiled, working night and day, so that we would not be a burden to any of you" (2 Thess. 3:6–8).

Paul practiced being a role model as a primary strategy for Christian leadership. He was willing to shoulder the burden of living in such a way that others could grow closer to Jesus by emulating him. He trained other leaders to do the same thing. As a Christian leader, you have both the privilege and responsibility of being a role model. Christian leadership isn't detached management of people and processes. It's engaging people personally, with vulnerability and authenticity, so they learn how to live the Christian life by watching you. Christians are specifically exhorted to watch you and imitate you: "Remember your leaders who have spoken God's word to you. As you carefully observe the outcome of their lives, *imitate their faith*" (Heb. 13:7). So when you want your followers to make a significant commitment, set the pace by modeling what you ask others to do. They *are* watching!

When it comes to modeling a challenging commitment, leaders must often set the pace through public acts. When you want your followers to become more aggressive evangelists, they will be more inspired when you introduce your converts to the church than by sermons telling them to be more outreach oriented. When you want your followers to become more loving family leaders, they will be more motivated if your example of family leadership is producing healthy relationships with your spouse and children. And if you want them to give generously, they will be more motivated to give when they know you are setting the pace as a good steward.

David was a model of setting the pace in giving with a generous, public gift to help build the temple. After he outlined the governmental provision for temple building materials he had arranged, he added,

> "I now give my personal treasures of gold and silver for the house of my God over and above all that I've provided for the holy house: 100 tons of gold . . . and 250 tons of refined silver for overlaying the walls of the buildings. . . . Now who will volunteer to consecrate himself to the LORD today?"

> Then the leaders of the households, the leaders of the tribes of Israel, the commanders of thousands and of hundreds, and the officials in charge of the king's work gave willingly. For the service of God's house they gave 185 tons of gold and 10,000 gold drachmas, 375 tons of silver, 675 tons of bronze, and 4,000 tons of iron. Whoever had precious stones gave them to the treasury of the LORD's house. . . . Then the people rejoiced because of their leaders' willingness to give, for they had given to the Lord with a whole heart. King David also rejoiced greatly (1 Chron. 29:3–9).

David announced his gift publicly. His example motivated an outpouring of generosity by his followers. Great joy, both for David and the donors, marked the occasion when the offering was tallied. This story doesn't establish a rule that every leader should make every gift in public. That violates both the spirit and principle of giving as outlined in the New Testament. But this story does establish this principle: Public giving by a leader can motivate generous giving among followers. There are occasions, like a building campaign or special missions offering, when a leader should model a challenging commitment by making a public gift. Doing so is biblical and may motivate a dramatic response.

One pastor, with a congregation of three hundred attendees and an annual budget of about $350,000, challenged his church to give $2 million over three years to fund a major building project. He announced his family would give $25,000 toward the project. Church members were surprised because this was a significant sacrifice for a person with their pastor's salary. Fund-raising experts projected this church could raise about $1 million (three times its annual budget) with a successful campaign. Then God came to church! The people committed to give $2 million and actually gave just over $2 million in the following three years. The spirit of sacrifice was evident in both the nature and amount of the gifts received—cash, land, stocks, jewelry, etc. While many factors produced this remarkable giving experience, the leader's willingness to publicly model a challenging commitment was certainly one key element.

Healthy Modeling

Two important words for role modeling in Christian leadership are transparency and authenticity. These two concepts are two sides of an important coin—the coin of *appropriately* revealing your motives and actions to encourage and motivate your followers. Transparency implies freedom from pretense or deceit. Being transparent means your life is visible and accessible. Authenticity means genuine character, without counterfeit. Being authentic means when people see you, they see the real you. You aren't playing the role of a Christian leader; you are a Christian leader. And you are the same person in every setting—home, church, and community.

Transparency and authenticity are essential qualities for being a role model. Establishing a pattern of transparent, authentic living is also essential to modeling a challenging commitment. You can't simply "turn on" transparency and authenticity when you want to inspire people by your example. These qualities must be integral to you as a leader. Leadership isn't a role you play; it's the life you lead.

Leaders have various venues—speaking, preaching, teaching, writing, or counseling—in which transparency may involve proactively sharing their experiences. Transparency, revealing pertinent details about your life experiences, can be an intentional strategy to connect with your followers. You don't depend entirely on passive observation by your followers. Sharing your life story in these venues provides an opportunity to use your experiences as illustrations. Doing this can encourage your followers. Hearing your stories helps humanize your instruction, creates empathy with your hearers, and establishes common connections about shared problems. This kind of authentic sharing can be a vital tool in helping others.

But finding a balance in this area is essential. Presenting

yourself as a role model is a legitimate strategy. But drawing too much attention to yourself isn't helpful. Even when you do it the right way, with right motives, it can still be misunderstood. A few years ago our family was asked to be a panel and talk about family relationships. Along with our teenage children, we shared some of the communication problems we have faced, some of the struggles our family has been through, and the strategies we used to maintain our relationships. We shared several shortcomings and some of our successes. Most of the conference evaluations were affirming, but one lambasted the organizers for "putting a guilt trip on all of us by putting a 'perfect family' on the stage." Our transparency, sharing as honestly as possible, was encouraging to most people but offensive to a few who misheard our testimony as focusing only on our strengths.

While there are no foolproof rules for appropriate transparency, here are some suggestions for sharing your life as a role model for others.

Share your struggles, not only your successes.

Some leaders continually tell success stories, hoping to impress their followers and inspire them to better living. Considering what they reveal about themselves, a follower might conclude the leaders have a perfect marriage, perfect children, a perfect devotional life, along with perfect height and weight! No one is that good or has his life that together. Transparency involves sharing your weaknesses, struggles, and failures too. Most people identify more with your problems than with your successes. They already consider you successful, which is why they chose you as their leader.

They follow you because they aspire to be like you in some ways. Sharing your successes isn't necessary to establish your credibility or prove your spiritual moxie. Just the opposite is often true. Your credibility grows as your followers discover your human side. Even when you share your successes, be sure to include the process of how you achieved those victories, which probably involved confronting and overcoming a problem or weakness.

When my wife and I have casual discussions with seminary students, the conversation frequently turns to parenting. Our adult children are growing Christians with a healthy view of ministry involvement. Students often ask us, "How did you raise spiritually and emotionally healthy children in the fishbowl of a minister's home?" We are glad to talk about our experiences. But rather than brag on our parenting prowess, we talk more about mistakes we made and what we learned from them. And we made some big mistakes! Even when we talk about what we did right, we also try to share the process (often painful trial and error) of how we finally got it right. Hurting people turn to their leaders for answers. When we share our struggles, and how we worked through problems to achieve a level of success, our followers are encouraged and find hope to press on.

Share your struggles, not anyone else's.

Leaders sometimes use negative stories about their family, friends, counselees, or team members as examples for their followers. This is offensive at best, unethical at worst. Transparency is sharing *your* struggles, not those of others. This is particularly troublesome if a leader uses his spouse or children as negative illustrations when preaching or teaching. When using any family member as an illustration, be sure you have explicit permission to do so. And be sure your family member is the "hero" of the story. Using any negative information about a friend or colleague without his or her permission is also unacceptable.

One of my most embarrassing moments was narrating an illustration while preaching at a conference, naming a person in a past ministry setting—only to discover later the person was in the audience. An awkward moment, to say the least! My apology, while heartfelt, couldn't undo the embarrassment the person felt at having this story told in public. Make sure your attempts at transparency don't include exposing others in inappropriate ways.

Share to meet the needs of others, not your needs.

When you choose to be transparent, your motive matters. The right motive is the good of your followers. The wrong motive is anything hinting of self-adulation or self-promotion. Sharing personal information, even failures, is only helpful when a leader is focused on sharing from the perspective of helping followers instead of attracting attention (especially sympathy).

When a leader shares personal struggles with a wrong motive, a narcissistic catharsis takes place. The leader, under the guise of transparency, is really saying, "Look at me. Feel for me. Share my pain. Have sympathy for me." Narcissism is an inordinate focus on self. Catharsis is a purging of emotions for personal benefit. Leaders who reveal personal issues for these reasons embarrass themselves and make their followers uncomfortable. A more blatant form of this is a leader who continually talks only about successes or strengths. This is a more obvious form of narcissistic catharsis with similar results. Followers are embarrassed and uncomfortable, while leaders lose credibility. Followers instinctively know their leaders aren't always successful in every area of life. For leaders to attempt to create this illusion undermines their credibility.

Share appropriate details, not the gory details.

When a leader opens a window on his life, enough detail needs to be shared to communicate the message but not so much that unnecessary lines of decorum are crossed. For example, my life story includes difficult early years as the son of an alcoholic. That's really all that needs to be revealed to humanize my upbringing and connect my struggles with followers who may have similar experiences. There's no need to detail the kinds of problems we faced or describe specific violent acts. Revealing these details to a struggling counselee, for example, doesn't increase my credibility or contribute to establishing a relational connection. Allowing the person to know my empathy for him springs from a shared past experience is sufficient, without the gory details.

Sharing too many details can undermine your credibility because your followers may then question your discernment and judgment. It may also make them cautious about sharing intimate details with you, lest you put them on display in a future sermon or other public setting. One leader called his team together and told them about the spiritual impact of his recent hospitalization. That was fine. But he included details about catheters, the results of his loss of voluntary muscle control, and gastric problems that were simply unnecessary. His testimony was more exhibitionism than transparency. (TMI—too much information!)

This kind of so-called transparency doesn't contribute to leadership effectiveness. It reveals immaturity, bad judgment, and lack of discretion. These are unhealthy qualities that undermine your influence. Be transparent. But choose what you reveal and how you reveal it in appropriate ways.

Conclusion

As a Christian leader, you are a model for Christian service and growth. You are always on display, like a model on a perpetual runway. Your life is a transparent, authentic example of what it means to be a Christian. While you may occasionally choose to offer your experiences as an example, in reality you are always a living illustration for your followers—for good and bad.

Part of modeling is sometimes choosing to model a specific challenging commitment. There are times when you must make a public commitment in order to lead others to make private commitments. Don't shy from this responsibility or opportunity. The capacity to trust God, while others are watching, is a unique privilege. Doing it appropriately has an igniting effect and accelerates the faith response of others. It will sometimes cost you to do this, but pay the price for the good of your followers. It's worth it.

Early in the book of Acts, on several occasions, the Bible says Peter "stood up" in the process of leading the church (1:15; 2:14). Don't be afraid to stand up, to stand out, to live your life in front of people, and to thrust yourself to the forefront as a leader. Your example of strong, observable commitment is essential for your followers. They are watching and counting on you to set the pace.

Sharing genuine Christian fellowship, revealing yourself honestly and knowing your followers intimately, is one of the pleasures of Christian leadership. There is something liberating and profound about deep bonds formed through this process. That makes breaking those bonds painful. Yet, from time to time, God gives us new assignments. Making healthy transitions, being a role model even when leaving one ministry for another, requires delicate and deft leadership. Toward that goal we now turn our attention.

14

Moving to a
New Position

Ministry leaders usually accept a position with a commitment to stay in place for a long time, even for a lifetime. My dream, at twenty-one, was to become a pastor and stay with one church for forty years. That hasn't turned out to be God's plan. Yet each time I have changed leadership roles, I have still thought, *This is it. This will be my final job.* Most pastors and other Christian leaders have similar desires for permanence. We are pursuing a calling, not building a career. We accept an assignment from God and plant ourselves to pursue it passionately. We aren't trying to move up a spiritual corporate ladder. Most leaders aren't looking for a perpetual greener pasture. We are more focused on improving the one we have.

Yet leaders do change ministry positions, roles, and locations. Leaders, just like their followers, are always growing, maturing, and changing. Ministry settings are also in a state of flux. This combination of personal growth and shifting ministry contexts can result in the need for a change to a new assignment. God has a remarkable way of bringing along a new opportunity at just the right time when it's best for all concerned—for you, your family, the place you are leaving, and the place where you are going. This chapter is about *leaving well*—about managing the painful process of transition caused by your departure.

This chapter is narrowly focused on leaving well as part of a healthy resignation or retirement. It assumes you have made a God-directed decision to leave and it's the right decision at the right time. This chapter isn't about making that decision, enduring a forced termination, leaving a ministry for the wrong reasons, leaving without God's clear direction, or leaving for a new setting to satisfy your ego. It's about leaving well when you have made the right decision, at the right time, for the right reason. Even when all these "rights" are in place, it's still possible to leave in wrong ways that harm your ministry organization and hamper your future leadership effectiveness. Good leaders minimize those results.

Several years ago I was discussing an effective pastor with a mentor who had known the other man for many years. We celebrated his success in his current church, as well as the health of the church he had formerly led in another part of the state. My friend said, "One of the things I most admire about him is he has a great 'after I left story' in his former church. His leaving was a blessing to two churches—the one he left and the one he now leads." Having a good "after I left story" was a new concept to me. Over the years, watching some leaders leave well, and others not so well, has revealed common practices among those who left well. You can leave

well, and have a good "after you left story" as you implement the following best practices. Doing so will minimize
the painful aspects of transition for you, your followers, and
the people you will lead in your new assignment.

Write an Intentional Transition Plan

Once you decide to leave, more is required than submitting a letter of resignation and making an announcement to
the church or organization. Such an abrupt exit, without a
thorough transition plan for you and your organization, is
irresponsible. If you can depart without a plan for managing
your absence, maybe you weren't that necessary in the first
place. The departure of an effective leader mandates a thorough, written transition plan. Your plan should facilitate the
processes for your departure and for moving the organization
forward while it searches for a new leader. This plan should
include the following five elements:

1. A communication plan to inform the appropriate
   people, in the appropriate sequence, of your plan to
   leave.
2. A teaching plan (speaking, preaching, or writing) to
   address appropriate issues like trusting God through
   change, working through the grief process, not
   fearing the unknown, or other subjects related to
   the transition.
3. A secession plan to assign your job responsibilities to
   people who will cover them after you are gone.
4. A selection plan to initiate the process of searching
   for the person who will replace you.

5. A timetable that includes dates when communication will be released, when speeches or sermons will be delivered, when persons will be trained to assume your duties, when your responsibilities will be transferred to others, and checkpoints in the search for your replacement.

The transition plan should take into account church or organizational policies and governance practices, particularly as they relate to the timetable for specific events. Part of this plan will be developed privately—like setting the date to tell key leaders about your impending departure. But other aspects of the plan should be negotiated with your leadership team. The plan then becomes the framework to guide others through the time leading to your departure and the months following, until the transition to a new leader is complete.

Keep the nature of a transition plan in mind. It's a framework for making decisions about your departure and the future of your organization. A transition plan doesn't answer all the questions but rather identifies the questions and lays out a path to the answers. Your transition plan should include necessary decisions and who will make those decisions. For example, a poor transition plan created by a departing pastor would be, "After October 1, Rev. Smith will assume the preaching duties while the church searches for a new pastor." A better statement would be, "By October 1, the deacons will identify and select a person to assume the preaching duties for the church." This second statement identifies the problem, assigns it to a person or group responsible for the decision (in that particular church/organization), and establishes the date by which it must be solved. A good transition plan has a series of action statements that become a checklist to manage the transition.

An underlying assumption of making this plan is that you will do your job to the end of your tenure, not just to the day you decide to leave. Some leaders decide to leave and pour all their energy into preparing for their next assignment. Resist this temptation. One laywoman said, "When a leader leaves, too often he is like a school-age child who starts summer vacation two weeks before the term ends!" While focusing on your future position is enticing, the people you are currently leading are still depending on you. Your final responsibility as the leader of the organization you are leaving is to ensure the best transition possible.

Making a transition plan raises the issue of how long the transition should take. The plan should cover two aspects—your personal transition and your organization's collective transition. In the case of a resignation, your personal plan will probably cover a few weeks or perhaps a month or two. Retirement often calls for a different model. In that case, your personal transition may take longer and may parallel the organization's transition plan for many months. Some long-tenured leaders announce their retirement a year or more in advance and work alongside their replacement to ensure a smooth transition. The length of your transition plan should be determined by the unique needs of each situation. But keep this general principle in mind—once you announce you are leaving, you need to leave sooner rather than later. Too long a transition is usually more problematic than too short.

The transition plan may also outline events that will take place after you leave. For example, for organizations that provide housing for their leaders, a part of the transition plan may be remodeling or repairing the residence for the next occupant. The corporate aspects of the transition may take place over a much longer time frame than the time for your personal transition. The corporate plan may cover several months while your personal plan is more compact. Making a good plan won't eliminate all painful aspects of the change, but it will mitigate many that would otherwise be unnecessarily problematic.

Overcommunicate about Everything

During transition people feel vulnerable. They are unsettled and want things to stabilize as quickly as possible. To facilitate this, to provide premature closure and a sense of being in control, well-meaning people will create erroneous scenarios about your decision to leave and how the transition will unfold. Sometimes those conclusions will astound you! Remember this leadership corollary: "In the absence of information, people will make it up." Your followers aren't being deceitful or duplicitous. People simply abhor uncertainty. They want to know what is happening to them, what is going to happen to them, and when it's going to happen. If you don't communicate the answers to those questions early and often, your followers will draw their own erroneous conclusions based on partial information and speculate about the future to everyone's detriment.

The first step in your communication plan is to inform the key leader in your organization. Start with the chairman of your board or leadership team (however your church or ministry is structured). If you report to another employee, inform your supervisor. Letting the person who will be most responsible for managing your departure know about it first is both courteous and strategic. It gains favor with the person you will work closely with during your personal transition and who will probably manage much of the corporate transition.

The second step is to inform your leadership team or key personnel. This might involve a governing board, personnel committee, or leadership peers. Telling this many people, however, is tantamount to a public announcement (even among the most tight-lipped groups). Share the information with this group a short time before you make your public announcement.

The third step is to inform key friends or trusted colleagues. There are always a few people you want to inform personally—not in an announcement, e-mail, or letter. Again, time this to occur just before your public announcement. Obviously, once you tell these two groups—your leadership team and key friends—the news will begin to spread about your departure. In some cases, because of turmoil this might create, it may be best to compress this timetable to a few hours rather than a few days.

Finally, tell your church or organization by communicating personally and simultaneously with as many people as possible. This might involve a public announcement, along with a mass e-mail sent out just after the announcement and a notice posted on your organization's Web site. The first communication should focus on the reasons you are leaving, appreciation for the organization's contribution to your life, the general timetable for your departure, and that a transition plan is being created and will be communicated soon. Trying to roll out the transition plan in the initial announcement is too much information to assimilate. It's better to make a resignation announcement (through the media mentioned above) and then post, publish, e-mail, or mail the transition plan a few days later.

Even if you work through this process in an orderly fashion with clear information at each step, communication (particularly when people are emotionally unsettled) can be garbled. For this reason, it's important to overcommunicate about these issues. You will need to repeat your reasons for leaving, your affirmation for the organization, and the highlights of the transition plan over and over again in various venues from coffee shops to hallway conversations to e-mails to newsletters. Hearing the same talking points reassures your followers and gives them a continuity of understanding as they piece together their thoughts about the future. Particularly in churches, where attendance is sporadic and church publications not always read carefully, you will need to repeat your core transition details over and over.

As you develop your resignation statement, be honest about your reasons for leaving. Avoid clichés. People already know "The Lord is leading me" and are dubious about "I really don't want to go, but I must." Just be honest. If you are going to a larger leadership opportunity, say so. If you have changed and no longer fit where you are, say you are going to a place where you feel you will fit better. If you are moving to care for aging parents or improve the health of your spouse, don't be afraid to say so. The truth will come out eventually, so go ahead and make it part of your resignation communication. While being truthful, also be discreet about personal or family reasons that might embarrass others or disclose confidential information related to the reasons for your relocation.

Also leave out any negative attacks or derogatory remarks about your current setting or any person who is part of your current ministry. Your resignation announcement isn't your final salvo to set the record straight, get even with your critics, or say something you just want to get off your chest. While tension, frustration, or disappointment may be a part of the reason you are leaving, it's not the time to vent those emotions. There is a time to attempt to resolve those issues—but when you are resigning isn't it.

Define Your Future Relationship

Many people where you currently serve love you and will miss your leadership and friendship. The assumption for them is (and possibly for you as well) those relationships will remain the same after your departure. That assumption is both impractical and unhealthy. Part of leaving well is defining the nature of your future relationship to your former ministry organization. This can be particularly important, and sometimes sticky, when leaving a church leadership role.

Six years after being the founding pastor of a new church, I resigned to lead a denominational ministry. My position change didn't, however, require our family to relocate. We lived in the same house, in the same community, and—ultimately—stayed in the same church. We were able to do this for two reasons: First, my future role was defined explicitly as part of the church's transition plan (developed according to the model presented earlier). I agreed to leave the church completely for one year *and* could return only with the permission of the new pastor. I also agreed I would never take any future leadership role in the church. After a year, I received our new pastor's permission to return. He made it possible for us to continue in the church and, as the years went by, assume some ministry roles (always with his approval). Today, many years later, we are still good friends.

The second reason we were able to return was the security and maturity of our new pastor. He not only facilitated my continued involvement in the church but eventually employed my wife on his staff. He is a secure, competent leader who made our transition much easier. This raises a corollary issue. When you arrive at a new leadership position, except in the case of a start-up position, you will have a predecessor. The way you relate to him or her is significant. Your followers will respect you more if you honor your predecessor and facilitate a healthy relationship with him or her, and between your followers and their former leader.

When you leave for a new position, applying two key principles will help define healthy relationships with your former followers. First, when you leave, really leave. Even though I came back after a while, I left completely for one year. This allowed the church to separate emotionally from me as the founding pastor and bond with their new pastor. Second, if you return for any purpose (even for a casual visit), clear it with the new pastor first. Almost ten years later, after we had moved to another state, a young woman asked me to return and participate in her wedding. Even after ten years, I officiated at the ceremony only after securing permission from the pastor. Remember, when you leave—leave. And don't return without the permission and blessing of the current pastor.

When you resign or retire, don't reject your followers or ask them to reject you. But redefine your relationship.

Define the new relationship explicitly, with specific examples, as part of your departure process. You should continue as their friend but not as their pastor, minister, leader, confidant, counselor, or adviser. Friend, yes! Ministry leader, no. Making this clear may seem harsh, but in the long run it will facilitate their healthy relationships with you and your healthy relationship with their current leader.

Manage the Grieving Process

She was a challenging person to serve in my first pastorate. For more than five years, my performance and her expectations seldom connected. She wasn't shy about pointing out my shortcomings. But in the year before my resignation, her adult daughter endured a significant health crisis and died. Through that process, and particularly one crucial night, I provided pastoral care for her family. We bonded more profoundly than I was aware. When I announced my resignation, she confronted me with tears and said, "I can't believe you're leaving when you've just now learned how to be my pastor!"

Three things surprised me about that exchange—the tears, the regrets, and her claiming me as her pastor. Over the next few weeks, while we worked through our transition plan, the emotions people demonstrated surprised me. I learned a resignation (or retirement) is the death of a relationship, producing grief for many people. The grief process has been described with various stages or phases including shock, anger, denial, bargaining, and adjustment. When you leave a ministry setting by resignation or retirement, you can expect your followers to move through these phases. Because you are leaving, you may not be around for the adjustment phase and may be subjected primarily to anger, denial, and bargaining. Anger is expressed when people say things like, "I can't believe you are leaving us. I don't understand why our church isn't good enough for you. I always knew you would go somewhere else." Denial and bargaining sound like this, "I knew we should have paid you more. I knew we should have followed you more willingly. What can we change to get you to stay with us?"

Part of your responsibility in leaving well is helping people process those feelings and move toward adjustment to the "new normal" of your absence and the promise of a new leader coming. The first step in this process is expecting a grieving response from people. Don't be surprised, or react negatively, when people express shock, anger, denial, or attempt bargaining. It will help if you remember people are grieving a death, the death of a relationship. Treat them as you would people in a pastoral-care situation grieving the death of a loved one.

You can help people process their grief in two venues— personal conversations and public presentations. During personal conversations, as in other pastoral care dialogue, help people talk through their feelings the same way you would in a grief-counseling situation. The situation is somewhat unique in that you, rather than a deceased person, are the object of the grieving response. This means emotions like anger may be directed toward you. Resist the temptation to take any of this personally.

You can also help people process their grief through sermons, speeches, and other communication venues. How can you do this? Acknowledge the grief process is happening.

Help define and categorize what people are feeling. Describe your emotional process as a model for how they might work through their feelings. Lay out biblical insights to help them understand their feelings and gain an accurate perspective on the situation. Don't be morbid, centering every message or communiqué during the transition on the negative emotions people are feeling. Acknowledge them, help people deal with them, and move them toward a more positive perspective on the future.

Part of helping people work through this process is managing both their negative and positive emotions. We have focused thus far mostly on negative emotions. When you resign or retire, you should expect a wide range of emotional response. Some will celebrate with you. Tears will flow—tears of sorrow and joy, sometimes intermingled. Many leaders are matter-of-fact people, task-oriented doers, who aren't comfortable when too much emotion is expressed. Part of leaving well is allowing emotions to flow—both yours and your followers'—so feelings are resolved, rather than suppressed. This can be draining, but it is nonetheless essential for bringing closure to relationships ending by your leaving.

Another aspect of bringing closure is reconciling broken relationships. Every attempt should be made to leave on good terms with everyone. While this is unlikely, it's still a worthy goal. Your transition isn't the time to get even, say what you always wish you could have said, or take vengeful actions toward others. One pastor, who lived in a parsonage, had a recurring frustration with the church he served. The church refused to maintain the parsonage, thus causing his wife and family to feel devalued. When they moved, they left the parsonage in bad repair to, in his words, "force the church to do something about it for the next guy." While the end may have been understandable, the means were inappropriate. Leaving is a time for reconciling, making things right, and leaving a positive last impression of your leadership. Don't make leaving even more painful by saying or doing things that leave a bad last impression.

Express and Receive Appreciation

Most leaders, when they leave for another role, want the whole process to be over without too much hoopla. Don't devalue, however, the need for closure events—an official end to your tenure. This might include an office party, appreciation dinner or banquet, recognition in a public service or ceremony, or giving and receiving expressions of appreciation. While it's good to be appreciated, you should also express gratitude for the opportunity to lead, the loyalty of your followers, and their accomplishments during your tenure. No leadership relationship is perfect, but good can be found in almost every situation. Express the positive aspects of the contribution your followers have made to you, your family, and your future.

While you should *not* expect parting gifts, graciously receive whatever is offered—both humorous gifts as well as those with sentimental or real value. One of my favorite gifts, received after resigning in the Northwest to move to California, is a baseball home plate with a superimposed picture of the staff in my former organization. They all signed the plate under the inscription, "From your home team." Another important gift is a box of appreciation letters and a large, needlepoint commemorating my first pastorate. Still another meaningful memento is a plaque commemorating my pastoral leadership in the church we planted.

Besides sentimental gifts, generous donors and ministry organizations sometimes give cash gifts to help with personal transition expenses. While receiving gifts may feel awkward for leaders more accustomed to giving accolades than receiving them, exchanging gifts is an important closure experience for people in most cultures. Over time, the value of these gifts increases and their sentiment becomes more meaningful. Take time to express appreciation and receive appreciation from others. It is part of closing the loop on the grieving process and soothing some of the pain of leadership transition.

Care for Your Family

Many leaders have a family—a spouse and children who are also part of the leaving process. When a leader decides to relocate, his family is greatly impacted. Family members are forced to change jobs, schools, friends, and houses. Unless you are employed by a church, they must also find a new church, new ministries, and establish new relationships for evangelism and ministry in a new community. While you, as the leader, may be very excited about moving to a new opportunity, your family may not share your enthusiasm. And, even if they do, different members of your family may have different levels of adjustment in moving to a new setting. For example, one of your children may move easily into a new school, find new friends, and quickly establish a new identity while another child may struggle with one or more of these issues. What can you do to mitigate the challenge of relocating for your family?

First, in appropriate ways, involve the entire family in the process to relocate. You must certainly include your spouse in the decision-making process. While there might be an unusual exception, it's almost inconceivable that a leader would make a decision to relocate without the full support of the spouse. God often works through a spouse to clarify if he is leading forward—or not! My wife and I have learned the hard way that when we lack unity and press ahead independently, we almost always make bad decisions. We have three "getting a dog" stories in our family's history that are humorous reminders of this principle. While getting a dog isn't nearly as serious as changing leadership positions, our three fiascoes remind us how important unity is in our decisions. Each time, one or the other of us got a dog without the other's input. And each time it was a disaster! Now, when we consider big decisions, we sometimes joke, "Let's not make another 'dog' decision. Let's get together on this one."

Involving children is also an important part of deciding to change leadership positions. Determining the best way to do this will be different for each family depending on the children's age and maturity. For example, we once moved when our children were all under five years old. We explained what we were doing and why, answered their questions, allayed their concerns, but didn't allow their opinion to dictate the decision. We knew, as preschoolers, they would ultimately be happy if they were safely close by two parents who were happy. Since we were in complete unity, and quite excited about the move, we knew our children would take their emotional cue from us and adjust well.

The next time we considered a leadership change requiring relocation, our oldest child was in college and the other two were in high school. This time we brought the children into the decision-making process and heard their opinions about the issues. We worked with them on their questions and concerns. We had many family conversations about whether we should move and what the move would be like if we did. While the ultimate decision was between my wife and me, we valued our children's input and wanted them to have a sense of unity with us in the process. We worked to make it a family decision we could all embrace.

Including your spouse and children in the decision-making process is important, but it isn't the end of caring for your family during transition. Your family's transition will continue for many months after your actual position change or relocation. When you write your personal transition plan, it should include helping your family adjust for about a year after you arrive in your new position. As a leader focused on the challenges and rewards of organizational leadership and the relationships naturally produced through your work, you may find it hard to realize other family members are transitioning more slowly (and more painfully). But they often are. Be sure your transition plan involves paying attention to adjustments made by every member of your family. As the first year unfolds, be sure each person receives the help and care he or she needs to make a successful transition. Be patient. Your pastoral care for the people who matter most— your family—can alleviate some of their pain in relocating.

Conclusion

Moving to a new ministry position can be exciting and painful, sometimes at the same time. It's full of promise for the future and nostalgia about the past. It's a complicated unraveling of current relationships and defining them for the future, while at the same time initiating a whole new set of relationships. It may involve financial change—more income or less income—and the necessary family adjustments. Changing leadership positions, especially if it involves relocation, impacts every member of your family. While some may look forward to the change, others may regret or resist it. All these variables, and countless others, require good leadership. A significant leadership challenge is managing transition successfully, moving yourself, your family, and two different organizations forward simultaneously. It's a hard task, but by understanding some of the core dynamics of the process, you can implement procedures to maximize your effectiveness as a transition leader and minimize the painful side of resignation, relocation, or retirement.

Dealing with the issues in this book, including this one, can be depressing. Yet, God wants his leaders to press through the pain and find joy in leading his people. Toward that end, God has given us a special gift—hope!

15

Hope—God's Gift to Hurting Leaders

While leadership is often painful, God has given you a great gift—hope. Hope is the confident expectation of a positive future in spite of your present circumstances. No matter how harsh your critics, how lonely your setting, how difficult your followers, or how serious your mistakes, God will advance his kingdom and accomplish his purposes. Your confident expectation—your hope for a positive future—rests on God's purposes and resources, not yours.

Hope is grounded in and emerges from your relationship with Jesus Christ. The scope of this is outlined in the New Testament. First, hope is only possible through a relationship with Jesus—"We recall, in the presence of our God and Father, your work of faith, labor of love, and endurance of hope in our Lord Jesus Christ" (1 Thess. 1:3). Second, hope is possible because of the Resurrection—"Blessed be the God and Father of our Lord Jesus Christ. According to

His great mercy, He has given us a new birth into a living hope through the resurrection of Jesus Christ from the dead" (1 Pet. 1:3). Finally, hope will ultimately be fulfilled in Jesus's return—"Therefore, get your minds ready for action, being self-disciplined, and set your hope completely on the grace to be brought to you at the revelation of Jesus Christ" (1 Pet. 1:13). As Christian leaders, we have biblical promises and theological resources centered on Jesus that produce hope. Because of our relationship with Jesus, confidence in his resurrection, and the reality of his second coming, we have a confident expectation of a positive future—no matter our present leadership challenges.

Paul had his share, perhaps more than his share, of leadership challenges (see 2 Cor. 11:22–33 for a refresher on his résumé). He summarized his struggles and the hope he maintained when he wrote, "For we don't want you to be unaware, brothers, of our affliction that took place in the province of Asia: we were completely overwhelmed—beyond our strength—so that we even despaired of life. However, we personally had a death sentence within ourselves so that we would not trust in ourselves, but in God who raises the dead. He has delivered us from such a terrible death, and He will deliver us; we have placed our hope in Him that He will deliver us again" (2 Cor. 1:8–10). As a leader, Paul faced "affliction" and felt "completely overwhelmed." He and his team were tested so far "beyond [their] strength" they "despaired of life." The situation was so oppressive they felt "a death sentence" had been placed on them. Yet, they maintained "hope in Him." Their hope was grounded in their relationship with Jesus and their experience with his past deliverance from difficult circumstances.

Been there? Are you there now? You have the same hope. No matter how tough your circumstances, you can trust Jesus to deliver you. Sometimes, he delivers *from* problems. Most of the time, he will deliver you *through* your difficulties. But you will be delivered! If not, the ultimate conclusion (especially in places where Christian leaders work in dangerous situations) is deliverance through martyrdom. But even in those cases "living is Christ and dying is gain" (Phil. 1:21). Death is the ultimate deliverance, the ultimate hope, for Christian leaders. In every circumstance, in life or death, it's possible to maintain hope in Jesus Christ. But when you are discouraged, how do you bring your emotions in line? Are there spiritual perspectives and practices that invigorate hope? Yes! Here are some strategies you can implement.

The first pathway to hope is changing your perspective on your struggles. Rather than seeing them as random, painful, out-of-control acts—recognize God's hand using them to accomplish his purpose of shaping the character of Jesus in you. God's ultimate purpose is to conform you "to the image of His Son" (Rom. 8:29). His purpose for you is character development—changing you into a new person who is more and more like Jesus. God specializes in using difficulties to shape us in positive ways. Paul wrote, "We also rejoice in our afflictions, because we know that affliction produces endurance, endurance produces proven character, and proven character produces hope" (Rom. 5:3–4). Note the progression: affliction leads to endurance, which leads to character development, which leads to hope. This means when your leadership circumstances are painful, God is at work. He allows affliction to create endurance. As you endure, character is forged in the crucible of difficult experiences. And when the process reaches its ultimate conclusion, your certainty about a positive future rests entirely on God. Your hope doesn't rest on your abilities, capabilities, or any results you thought you could produce. So the first step toward hope is changing your perspective. Your tough situation isn't hopeless; it's the anvil on which God is pounding out every ounce of self—self-trust, self-effort, self-sufficiency, and self-confidence about the future. Your leadership challenges are the path to hope—a confident expectation of *God's* future being fulfilled in your church or organization.

A second pathway to hope is the Bible. Paul wrote, "For whatever was written before was written for our instruction, so that through our endurance and through the encouragement of the Scriptures we may have hope" (Rom. 15:4). When your situation seems hopeless, turn to the Bible for encouragement. Many leaders, as they become discouraged, spend less time with the Bible instead of more. When you are facing a tough situation, redouble your commitment to devotional Bible reading. Do Bible studies about characters who faced situations similar to yours or even more challenging problems. Study heroes and heroines in the Bible for inspiration in facing arrogant giants, fiery furnaces, wicked rulers, and marauding armies. Memorize verses or passages reminding you of God's love and care, his ability to bring good out of evil, and the spiritual resources you have for hope in Jesus, his resurrection, and his return. If you are not sure where to start, just memorize the passages used in this chapter. That's a good beginning!

A third pathway to hope is the filling of the Holy Spirit. Paul wrote a benediction-like desire for believers to have hope, "Now may the God of hope fill you with all joy and peace in believing, so that you may overflow with hope by the power of the Holy Spirit" (Rom. 15:13). Hope comes from being filled with the Holy Spirit. To be filled with the Spirit means being controlled by the Spirit. When you are controlled by a spirit of fear, you are filled with a spirit of fear. The same with discouragement: When you are controlled by it, you are filled with a spirit of discouragement. *Filled* equals controlled. *Controlled* equals filled. It's important to seek filling from the Holy Spirit, not allowing negative emotions to dominate your perspectives or decisions.

As Christian leaders, we have the capacity to be filled or controlled by the Holy Spirit. The means to filling is simple: Ask for the filling of the Spirit and then take action by faith. These two realities are two sides of the same spiritual coin. The filling of the Spirit is only experienced in the context of faith-induced action. When you pray for the filling of the Spirit for witnessing, for example, the filling only becomes evident when you open your mouth and begin speaking the gospel. Taking action in faith is tacking into the wind of your leadership challenges with the confident assurance God will sustain you. Hope emerges when the filling of the Spirit is revealed through specific actions based on a confident expectation of a positive outcome. The filling of the Spirit prompts faith-based action, not emotional exuberance or outbursts.

A final pathway to hope is changing your perspective on the difficult followers who are causing you so much pain. These people, these unruly sheep you are trying to lead forward, are part of your hope for the future. Paul wrote, "For who is our hope, or joy, or crown of boasting in the presence of our Lord Jesus at His coming? Is it not you? For you are our glory and joy!" (1 Thess. 2:19–20). What does this mean?

It means your followers are your ultimate product and your ultimate satisfaction. When you appear before the Lord in heaven, you won't point to buildings you built, organizations you led, money you raised, sermons you preached, classes you taught, or projects you finished on time and on budget to validate your leadership. You will stand before him with people you have led to faith in Jesus and trained to live for him. Your ultimate product as a leader is people—those you lead to faith in Jesus and those you help become more like Jesus. People are your product.

Leadership pain is often caused by followers. It's easy to resent them for their immaturity or rebelliousness. We are easily exasperated at their foibles and failures. In those times, ask God to renew your love for the sheep, even the ones that bite. Ask God for fresh perspective on the value of his children, all of them. Ask him to renew your love for those you lead. When you stand before the Lord, you will look around at the people who join you there and present them as your hope, glory, and joy. Start practicing that perspective now.

While serving as a pastor, my churches had special services on Christmas Eve. One of my favorite formats was a come-and-go service led by deacons every hour, on the hour, throughout the afternoon and evening. My role was training others to lead those services, including serving the Lord's Supper, and then watching them lead worship. During those services, I would sit in the back of the sanctuary and watch families come and go. As the day unfolded, my thoughts were an annual review of the spiritual condition of my followers. Some had lost spouses, some had new babies, some were newly married, and others now empty nesters. Some had retired or lost jobs. Others had been promoted or their businesses were thriving. A few marriages had been saved, and usually one or two lost. Teenagers, feigning indifference, worshipped with their parents. Recently baptized children, wide-eyed with wonder, participated in the Lord's Supper for the first time. Counselees who had revealed their secret sins came, as did others unaware of the private wars of fellow believers standing next to them.

Each time I promised myself I would observe dispassionately and only stay for part of the day. But each year without fail, I lingered long with heartfelt compassion for the people coming to worship. Feelings welled up as the privilege of being their undershepherd, their pastor, overwhelmed me. Before long, hours of quietly worshipping and thanking the Lord for allowing me to lead his people had passed. Leaders love their followers. Deep down, a profound passion drives us to serve those entrusted to us. From time to time, however, we need experiences to remind us of this and reconnect our hearts with God's heart for his people. Particularly when followers create painful circumstances, they are hard to love. But love them we must! They are our glory and joy. The only eternal result of our leadership efforts is standing before the Lord with these unruly sheep and presenting them to him.

May God give you the grace to lead, even when it's painful, and the grace to give your life for God's people who are depending on you to help them become what they don't know they can be, go where they don't know they can go, and do what they could never otherwise dream of accomplishing. Lead on, full of hope, even when you find yourself on the painful side of Christian leadership.

Notes

1. See my book *The Character of Leadership* for a more thorough discussion of this section (B&H Publishing Group, 2007).

2. Rick Warren, *The Purpose Driven Life* (Grand Rapids, MI: Zondervan, 2002), 17.

3. Lee Iacocca, *Iacocca: An Autobiography* (New York: Bantam, 1984), 50.

4. Joseph Rost, *Leadership for the Twenty-First Century* (Westport, CT: Praeger Publishers, 1991), 102.

Other must-have books by Jeff Iorg

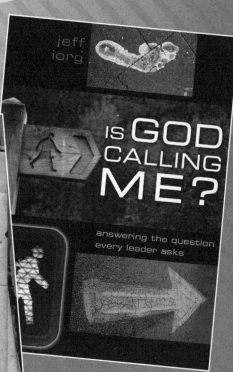

jeff iorg

IS GOD CALLING ME?

answering the question every leader asks

"God's purpose is first and foremost to shape you into the image of Jesus, the greatest leader of all time."
—Rick Warren, author of *The Purpose-Driven Life*

THE CHARACTER OF
LEADERSHIP
Nine Qualities that Define Great Leaders

JEFF IORG